WOLE S

Death and the
King's Horseman

with commentary and notes by
JANE PLASTOW

METHUEN DRAMA

Methuen Drama Student Edition

10 9 8 7 6 5 4 3

First published in Great Britain in this edition 1998
by Methuen Drama

Reissued with additional material and a new cover design in 2006; reissued
with a new cover design 2009

Methuen Drama
A & C Black Publishers Ltd
36 Soho Square, London W1D 3QY
www.methuendrama.com

Death and the King's Horseman first published in 1975 by Eyre Methuen Ltd
Copyright © 1975 by Wole Soyinka

Commentary and notes copyright © 1998, 2006 by Methuen Drama
Interview copyright © 1998 by Wole Soyinka and Alby James
The authors have asserted their moral rights

ISBN 978 0 413 69550 5

A CIP catalogue record for this book is available from the British Library

Typeset by Deltatype Ltd, Birkenhead, Merseyside
Printed and bound in Great Britain by CPI Cox & Wyman, Reading, RG6 8EX

Contents

Wole Soyinka: A Chronology

1934   Born 13 July, Akinwande Oluwole Soyinka, the
        second child of Samuel Ayodele and Grace Eniola
        Soyinka. Childhood spent in Abeokuta, Western
        Nigeria.

1938–   Educated at St Peter's School, Ake, Abeokuta.
43

1944–   Abeokuta Grammar School.
45

1946–   Attends the élite Government College in Ibadan,
50   where he writes sketches for his house drama group
        and wins prizes for his poems.

1950   Works as a clerk in Lagos. He continues his creative
        writing, has short stories read on national radio and
        pioneers radio drama.

1952   Enters University College, Ibadan, to study English,
        Greek and History. Performs leading roles in drama
        productions, co-founds a student fraternity, 'The
        Pyrates', edits a student magazine, *The Eagle*, and
        continues his creative writing.

1954   Goes to the UK to read for an honours degree in
        English at the University of Leeds. Acts with the
        University Drama Group, has short stories published
        in the student literary magazine, sings in the rag
        revue and shows an interest in politics.

1957   Awarded a 2:1 degree and starts an uncompleted MA
        course, focusing on the work of the playwright
        Eugene O'Neill. Begins writing two plays, *The Swamp
        Dwellers* and *The Lion and the Jewel*. The Royal Court
        Theatre in Sloane Square, London, reads *The Lion and
        the Jewel* and invites him to become a playreader.

1958   Moves to London. Works at the Royal Court,

teaches, and gets involved in broadcasting. He directs the Nigeria Drama Group in *The Swamp Dwellers* and then an evening of his work, including *The Invention*, at the Royal Court.

1960 Returns to Nigeria with a two-year Rockefeller research studentship to study drama in West Africa. *The Swamp Dwellers* is given a radio broadcast and Soyinka completes two new radio plays, *Camwood on the Leaves* and *The Tortoise*; also a television play, *My Father's Burden*, and a stage play, *The Trials of Brother Jero*. He forms a theatre group – The 1960 Masks – and produces *A Dance of the Forests*, which raises questions about the future of the newly independent Nigerian state.

1961 Writes weekly scripts for the radio series *Broke-Time Bar* but leaves when he is forbidden to introduce social and political comment. He is commissioned to write a trilogy of plays for television, of which only the first, *The Night of the Hunted*, is transmitted. His poems are published in Sweden. He presents a film about Nigerian culture, *Culture in Transition*, which includes a version of his play *The Strong Breed*.

1962 Voices frequent criticisms of the government. Briefly lecturer in English at University College, Ife, but resigns for political reasons.

1964 Soyinka works actively for the overthrow of the government against a background of strikes and unrest. Produces *The Lion and the Jewel* during a season of Nigerian plays in English and Yoruba. The Orisun Theatre Group is formed.

1965 Soyinka produces another satirical revue, *Before the Blackout*, as political violence returns to the streets of Western Nigeria. In August, he premières a major new play, *Kongi's Harvest*, in the Federal Palace Hotel in Lagos. In September, in London for the Commonwealth Arts Festival, he reads his long poem 'Idanre' and attends rehearsals of his play *The Road* at the Theatre Royal, Stratford East, and the BBC

World Service recording of *The Detainee*. He is
appointed senior lecturer at the University of Lagos
and his novel *The Interpreters* is published. Violent
elections in Western Nigeria lead to victory for Chief
S. L. Akintola. Soyinka makes a radio tape disputing
the published results of the election, holds up the
broadcasting studio at gunpoint and insists on his
recording being played instead of Akintola's victory
address. He is arrested and charged but in court he is
acquitted on a technicality.

1967   In August Soyinka is detained without trial following
his political activities against the government during
the Biafran war. He writes about his experiences in
prison in *The Man Died*, published in 1972.

1969   On release in October 1969 he becomes director of
the School of Drama at Ibadan. He takes over a
production of *Kongi's Harvest* from Dapo Adelugba and
gives it an anti-General Gowon slant.

1970   Soyinka takes his theatre group from the School of
Drama to the Eugene O'Neill Center in America
where he presents the first production of *Madmen and
Specialists*.

1971–   Soyinka begins a self-imposed exile from Nigeria,
75   travelling and working around the world.

1973   Three plays are published: *The Trials of Brother Jero*,
The Metamorphosis of Brother Jero, and *The Bacchae of
Euripides* (a Yoruba version of this classic play, written
for Britain's National Theatre and given an
unimaginative first production there). Leeds University
awards him an Honorary Degree of Doctor of Letters
and *Season of Anomy*, a novel, is published.

1973–   Soyinka is Overseas Fellow at Churchill College,
74   Cambridge, where he writes the critical essays
contained in his book, *Myth, Literature and the African
World*, published in 1976. A centre for the study of
the literature of Africa and the Commonwealth is
started at his old university, Leeds.

1974   Goes to Accra in Ghana to become editor of

Transition, a leading critical magazine. He renames it *Ch'Indaba* and uses it to support socialist revolutionary movements in Africa and to attack the 'tin-pot tyrants'. He has a public disagreement with writers who consider him a reactionary in their mission to decolonise African literature. Soyinka joins with Dennis Brutus and others to establish the Union of Writers of African Peoples, and is elected Secretary-General.

1975   General Gowon is overthrown in a coup which brings Murtala Mohammad to power. Soyinka returns to Nigeria, takes up a professorship at the University of Ife. *Death and the King's Horseman* is published.

1976   Soyinka helps administer FESTAC, the Second Black and African Festival of Arts and Culture. Mohammad is assassinated and Olusegun Obasanjo takes over as Head of State. The oil boom economy, following the demonstration of power by the OPEC producers in 1973, has led to even greater corruption and inequalities. Soyinka comes under further intimidation because of his outspoken criticism. In December he directs the first production of *Death and the King's Horseman*.

1977   FESTAC is held in January. Soyinka completes *Opera Wonyosi*, an adaptation of Brecht's *Threepenny Opera*, which hits out at several African tyrants and their values. He is prevented from producing it in Lagos so he creates another theatre group, the Guerrilla Theatre Unit of the University of Ife, for which he writes short, popular dramas attacking government corruption and hypocrisy; these are performed in streets, markets and government premises.

1979   Soyinka directs and acts in *The Biko Inquest*, an edited version of the proceedings in a South African court following the death of Steve Biko in police custody. In the autumn Soyinka directs *Death and the King's Horseman* at the Goodman Theater, Chicago, its second professional production. It is well received and it transfers to the Kennedy Center in Washington DC. In October, Shehu Shagari wins the elections that return Nigeria to civilian rule. Soyinka creates the Oyo State Road Safety Corps, of which he later becomes Chairman.

1981   Soyinka is appointed Visiting Professor at Yale University. *Aké* is published, the first part of his autobiography, about his childhood in Abeokuta.

1982   Launching *Aké* in January, Soyinka uses the occasion to lambast Shagari's government and the leader's 'achievements': the killings and deportations; the despoliation of the country's wealth; the Bakolori Massacre; the subversion of the Kano state government; the destruction of the offices of *The Triumph* newspaper; the storming of an elected legislature; and the deaths at the hands of policemen of students, athletes and members of the Youth Corps. In March and April he presents a stage version of his radio play *Camwood on the Leaves* at the National Theatre in Lagos. On 18 August in Stratford-upon-Avon he delivers a lecture entitled 'Shakespeare and the Living Dramatist'. Later in the year, the half-hour play *Die Still, Dr Godspeak!*, about the influence of metaphysicians and parapsychologists in Nigeria, is transmitted on the African Service of the BBC World Service.

1983   The première on tour of *Requiem for a Futurologist*. He uses this tour to spread ideas contained in *Priority Projects*, a satirical revue which attacked the corruption, mismanagement and hypocrisy of the country. To reach an even wider audience, before the August national elections, Soyinka has the songs recorded and released on the 'B' side of a record called *Unlimited Liability Company*. Shagari is awarded victory again in the polls. Soyinka flies to London to use the British press and the BBC World Service to condemn the corruption in the election process. He predicts a coup or civil war. On 31 December

Shagari is overthrown in a coup which brings
Mohammadu Buhari to power.

1984   In February Justice Ademola-Johnson upholds part of
the petition brought by Femi Okunnu for damages
over *The Man Died* and issues an injunction against
further sales of the book. Soyinka's film, *Blues for a
Prodigal*, about a student seduced into recruiting for a
political party among his fellow students, is premièred.
In May his unsuccessful production of *The Road* opens
at the Goodman Theater in Chicago and in
December *A Play of Giants* is produced at Yale.

1986   Awarded Nobel Prize for Literature and one of
Nigeria's highest awards, the CFR (Commander of
the Federal Republic). As chairman of the Road
Safety Corps until 1993, Soyinka uses his high public
profile to criticise the Babangida military regime.

1988   *Art, Dialogue and Outrage* is published, a major
collection of essays on drama and literature. *Mandela's
Earth and Other Poems* is published.

1989   *Ìsarà: A Voyage Round Essay* is published, a fictional
study of Soyinka's father's friends.

1991   A new radio play *A Scourge of Hyacinths* is broadcast on
BBC Radio 4.

1992   An extension of the radio play, called *From Zia, With
Love*, is premiered in Siena, Italy. The play castigates
Nigeria's corrupt military regime.

1994   Publishes *Ibadan: The Penkelemes Years – A Memoir
1945–1965*, the third part of his autobiography.

1995   *The Beatification of Area Boy* is given its world première
at West Yorkshire Playhouse, Leeds, and published.

1996   Soyinka is forced into exile because of threats by the
military government of General Abacha.

1997   Soyinka is charged with treason by the Abacha
regime, and placed on trial *in absentia*. *The Beatification
of Area Boy* tours to Australia and Jamaica. Soyinka
becomes Woodruff Professor at Emory University,
USA.

Plot

Oyo, an ancient Yoruba city in Nigeria, 1944.

Scene One
The play begins thirty days after the death of the Alafin or
King of Oyo, on the day of his burial. Elesin, 'the King's
Horseman', 'a man of enormous vitality', is parading through
the streets, accompanied by drummers and his Praise-Singer.
He is preparing for the ritual which will enable him to
perform a willed suicide. This is his inherited duty, as the
King's Horseman has to lead his master through the
'transitional gulf', the passage between the world of the living
and that of the ancestors, in order to ensure continued
harmony between the worlds.

In the market-place, where the women are packing up their
wares for the day, Elesin greets the market traders. This is his
favourite place, the bustling centre of life in Yoruba towns.
The women adore the Horseman. When the Praise-Singer
warns him against being distracted from his sacred duty by
the women Elesin responds with the recital of the tale of the
Not-I bird. The Not-I bird represents the call of death and all
flee from him, but Elesin boasts that he alone is unafraid and
welcomes his imminent death.

Elesin pretends to be offended by the women, and when
they fearfully ask what they have done wrong, he demands
rich new clothes befitting his rank. Laughingly they give him
all he desires. Elesin then catches sight of a beautiful young
girl. He is a famous lover of women and now demands this
girl as his final wife. She is already betrothed to the son of
the chief of the market women, Iyaloja, and initially there is
reluctance to give such a girl to Elesin. However, Iyaloja then
decides that a man who is about to carry out such a huge
service for the community cannot be denied his wishes, and

she agrees to make immediate preparations for the wedding.

Scene Two

The veranda of the British colonial District Officer's house. Simon Pilkings and his wife, Jane, dance to a tango in *egungun* masquerade costumes. This is a blasphemy to any Yoruba as these masks represent the spirits of the ancestors. The Pilkings are going to wear them to a fancy-dress ball at the government residency that night. A native policeman, Sergeant Amusa, enters and recoils in horror when he sees the Pilkings' costumes.

Although a Muslim, Amusa is profoundly shocked at the Pilkings' desecration of the *egungun* masks and says he cannot 'talk against death to person in uniform of death'. Since he cannot speak to Pilkings, Amusa eventually agrees to write his report, and leaves. Because of the sergeant's poor English, Pilkings initially thinks the report means a ritual murder is about to take place. He questions his Christian servant, Joseph, who explains that Elesin must will his own death so that he can accompany the King to the ancestors. Throughout this scene the sound of the talking drums grows and dominates the background.

Pilkings and Jane discuss what they should do since suicide is illegal, and we learn that they have had disputes with Elesin before when they helped his son, Olunde, go to England to study medicine against his father's will. Throughout the scene Pilkings' racism and lack of respect for any religion become progressively clear.

As the drumming continues to grow louder Joseph is recalled to explain what the drums are saying. He tells them that the drums are celebrating both the marriage and the death of a great chief. Pilkings is unwilling to miss the ball, so he decides to send Amusa to arrest Elesin and lock him up in Pilkings' own house. We then learn that the reason Pilkings has been so reluctant to miss the ball is that the Prince, on a tour of the British colonies, will be the guest-of-honour.

Scene Three

In the market-place Sergeant Amusa and his constables arrive
to try to arrest Elesin. They are blocked by the market
women. The women then mock the policemen, deriding their
masculinity and their authority as lackeys of the white men.
The women say Elesin is consummating his marriage, not
committing any crime. To compound the confusion and
humiliation of the police the women's daughters' then take
over the mockery, parodying the behaviour of white people.
When they finally threaten to remove Amusa's shorts he beats
a hasty retreat.

Elesin appears bearing a blood-stained cloth which proves
that he has deflowered a virgin. He hears drums declaring
that the King's favourite horse and dog have been sacrificed
according to prescribed ritual. It is now time for Elesin to
begin his own journey towards death. With the assistance of
drummers, the women singing a dirge and the Praise-Singer,
Elesin begins to dance his way into the trance which will lead
to his death. The intensity of the trance deepens as the Praise-
Singer helps his master on until Elesin no longer has any
awareness of the surrounding world.

Scene Four

In contrast to the profound ritual taking place in the market-
place we are now in the tawdry splendour of the British
Residency. Couples in fancy-dress wait for the Prince. When
he arrives a band plays – badly – 'Rule Britannia'. The
ceremonial is undermined by the poor music and obvious
attempts of various couples to be chosen to be introduced to
the Prince. When the Pilkings are introduced they give a
parodic display of how the *egungun* masquers perform. This is
received with great amusement.

A footman hands a note to the Resident who extracts the
Pilkings from their audience with the Prince. The note is from
Amusa who describes his problems in arresting Elesin as an
'emergency'. Amusa appears in a state of disarray as a result
of his treatment by the market women but still refuses to talk

to Pilkings while he is wearing the *egungun* costume. Pilkings rushes off with two constables to try to stop Elesin committing suicide.

Jane is now approached by a young black man dressed in a western suit. It is Olunde, Elesin's son, who has just returned home after receiving a telegram telling him that the King is dead. Olunde and Jane have a long conversation about their different ideas of what constitutes duty. They discuss the war. A parallel to Elesin's suicide is unwittingly raised by Jane when she describes how a British ship's captain recently blew himself up with his ship in order to save hundreds of others. She does not recognise the significance of this story, but Olunde does. Olunde tries to explain the meaning of his father's death to Jane who only calls it 'feudalistic'. Olunde then questions the feudal nature of the ball. He expresses his horror at the war and the lies people are told about the terrible nature of that war. He is amazed at how hypocritical whites can be.

The drumming, which has gone on under the scene, rises to a crescendo and then changes rhythm. Olunde says calmly that the drums announce his father's death. Jane is horrified at what she sees as his callousness and screams at Olunde. An aide-de-camp appears and tries to send Olunde away but Jane apologises and the aide-de-camp reluctantly leaves. Olunde now wants to go to pay his last respects to his father's body, but before he can leave Pilkings reappears. He calls the aide-de-camp and asks him if an old cellar in the Residency, previously used to hold slaves, is still secure. He has a prisoner he wants to hold there under strong guard. Olunde is mystified by what might be going on when suddenly Elesin is heard bellowing in anger at his white captors. He runs on stage, having broken free, but comes to a standstill at the sight of his son. In his shame at his failure to carry out the ritual death Elesin begs Olunde to acknowledge him, but Olunde's rejection is total. He declares 'I have no father, eater of left-overs', and walks off stage leaving Elesin sobbing on the ground.

Scene Five

Elesin is seen manacled in the old, barred, slave cell, his wife
sitting with downcast eyes on the ground outside. The moon
shines. Pilkings, in police uniform, talks of the peace of the
night. He still has no understanding of Elesin and his role.
Elesin says that Pilkings has 'shattered the peace of the world
for ever'. The correct time for Elesin's death has gone, and
Elesin wonders if this is all part of a greater plan to disrupt
Yoruba harmony with the world. 'Did you think it all out
before, this plan to push our world from its course and sever
the cord that links us to the great origin?'

Pilkings tries to convey Olunde's apologies for insulting his
father, but Elesin is glad that Olunde has retained his Yoruba
sensibility despite spending time in the white man's world. He
believes Olunde will avenge his father's shame. Olunde has
told Pilkings he will come to seek his father's blessing before
he leaves again. He will come soon.

Pilkings is called away by his wife. Elesin turns to his bride
and confesses that he had wanted to blame her as well as the
white man for his weakness in failing to cross the transitional
abyss. But now the Horseman acknowledges that it was his
own longing for earthly things which drew him back from
completing his journey. There was a fundamental failure of
will.

Iyaloja arrives with a note from Olunde, and Elesin agrees
to see her since his shame cannot be made greater. Iyaloja
bitterly reproaches Elesin for betraying the trust put in him by
the people who had heaped honour on him during his life
precisely because of what he was to do for them. Elesin makes
a few weak excuses but has little fight left in him. Iyaloja
heralds a burden which is being brought to Elesin. The
burden is carried up the hill by the women. They enter
singing a dirge and bearing a large, cloth-wrapped object.
Elesin knows what it is, and asks to be released to carry out a
final duty. Pilkings, as ever, fails to understand and refuses
permission. The Praise-Singer sadly reproaches Elesin for his
vanity in thinking that he could accomplish his mission alone,
and for not calling for help when he realised his will was

weak.

Elesin orders the burden to be uncovered so that he may 'speak my message from heart to heart of silence'. Olunde is revealed. He has killed himself in order to do what he can to restore a rightful balance to the world and to restore the family honour. However, this alone is not sufficient. 'This young shoot has poured its sap into the parent stalk, and we know this is not the way of life.' Elesin stares in silence at the body. Then suddenly he strangles himself in his chains.

Iyaloja reproves Pilkings one last time, speaking to him as to a child who does not understand what he does. She then orders the bride to sprinkle ceremonial earth on the eyelids of her husband. Any hope now lies with the unborn child carried by the bride. Iyaloja orders the girl: 'Now forget the dead, forget even the living. Turn your mind only to the unborn.' The play closes with the women's dirge over the dead bodies of father and son.

Background

African theatre

Traditionally African theatre forms have drawn heavily on
music and dance cultures, along with mime, masquerade and
acrobatics. Story-telling is also seen as a vital root of
traditional African performance culture. In societies which
have been predominantly oral, stories provided not only
entertainment but also history and moral and social education.
What most of Africa did not have, until the advent of
widescale European colonisation in the late nineteenth century,
was much in the way of literary drama.

Some commentators argued that Africa had no pre-colonial
theatre simply because it did not have a literary drama form.
Others claimed that because much African performance was
based on religious ritual it could not be called theatre, since
that is a secular entertainment form. Increasingly, critics now
agree that Africa did have substantial secular performance
forms before colonisation and that ritual may also be
entertainment and not exclusively a form of worship. The idea
that only something approximating to Western established
drama forms can be called theatre is seen as merely a
Eurocentric definition which does not encompass a host of the
world's performance forms – or even many of the more avant-
garde theatrical modes now existing in the West.

The advent of colonialism did mean the import of
European performance forms to Africa. Particularly, for the
purposes of this study, European naturalist drama. In schools
and drama societies run on a European model this was the
theatre which was introduced to young Africans in the late
nineteenth and early twentieth centuries. In British colonies, as
higher education expanded, Shakespeare and Greek drama
were also introduced, but African forms were largely ignored
and seen as savage and inferior.

Early African attempts at writing drama were often inspired by Christianity, due to missionary influence. Later during the colonial period we see a small number of more secular African dramas, but these were usually imitative and, because they were subject to colonial censorship, their content often reflected messages the colonials wished to transmit. Modern African theatre dates back only to the immediate post-colonial period of the 1960s. At this time African playwrights such as Ama Ata Aidoo, Efua Sutherland and Wole Soyinka started to write new kinds of drama which brought together African and European theatrical forms and which spoke directly of African concerns.

What we see clearly in African theatre, both old and new, is that there is no concept of art purely for aesthetic reasons; it serves ritual/religious purposes or is socially or politically committed, and sees itself with an important role in debating how African societies should be run and how people should behave. This does not mean that such theatre is not aware of the importance of entertainment either, but entertainment alone is not sufficient in African theatre, which almost always has a functionalist aspect.

Consequently Soyinka is not exceptional in making his theatre politically engaged and concerned with moral questions. Playwrights such as the Nigerians, Femi Osofisan and Ola Rotimi, the Kenyan, Ngugi wa Thiong'o, or the South Africans, Percy Mtwa, Mbongeni Ngema and Athol Fugard, to mention only some of the most famous, have all continued the tradition of writing sharply critical political plays, even when this may entail considerable personal risk at the hands of intolerant governments. Such playwrights, like many other African writers, believe thay have a responsibility to serve the people through their art, and to continue the tradition of using the arts as a means of education.

The integration of music, dance and story-telling techniques with literary dramatic forms is widespread in modern African theatre. This syncretic approach imbues it with tremendous energy. It is also essential if African playwrights wish to reach wider audiences. Even today many Africans are illiterate and

unable to gain access to expensive forms of mass media.
Theatre is made accessible to many by utilising indigenous
performance forms, which speak to and of the people's
culture, where Western literary drama would be alien and
sterile.

Published African theatre is only the tip of the iceberg. In
many places traditional performances for weddings, harvest,
funerals, coming-of-age, etc., are still an integral part of
community life. Many groups write or devise their own
material which is never published, and even published
material may not be available widely because it has been
written in local languages. Nowadays there is a growing
community theatre movement in Africa. Devised theatre is
used to enable communities to debate topical ideas and to
speak in their own voices through the medium of
performance.

Wole Soyinka's work arises from, and is part of, this rich
cultural heritage. His work is rooted in Africa and African
performance traditions, but it has also been partly formed by
the Western theatrical modes to which he was introduced in
school and university. By combining both traditions,
playwrights like Soyinka have created new, dynamic kinds of
theatre, first for the use of Africans, but which can also be
accessible, useful and exciting for the rest of the world.

The Yoruba world view

The Yoruba are a major Nigerian ethnic group. They live in
the southwest of the country, and number some thirteen
million people. Their vision of the world has, in the twentieth
century, been overlaid by the influence of Christianity,
brought to Nigeria predominantly by British missionaries
during the colonial period. Many Yoruba people now have
religious and cultural lifestyles which accommodate both
indigenous beliefs and imported ideas from the West.

The Yoruba believe that life is much more inclusive than it
is commonly seen to be in the West. Man himself has three
states of being, all of which are linked and can influence each

other. These three states are the unborn, the living and the
ancestors, and all are linked by what Soyinka has called
variously a passage, an abyss or a transitional gulf.

The unborn inhabit their own spirit world from which they
come with their own consciousness to their parents. If they
don't like what they find they may choose to die as babies
and return to the spirit world. The world of the living is that
part of life that we all know. When someone dies, the Yoruba
– like many other African peoples – believe that he or she
goes to join the ancestors. The ancestors maintain intimate
links with the world of the living. Their descendants propitiate
them with regular offerings and rituals. In exchange the
ancestors can intercede for the living in their difficulties and
can be approached for guidance. To have children is therefore
extremely important to any Yoruba, as without the constant
replenishment of descendants the ancestors would have no one
to honour them and would effectively die. It is also important
to an understanding of *Death and the King's Horseman* to realise
that earthly rank and honour are thought to be reflected in
the realm of the ancestors. A great leader or warrior will be a
powerful ancestor, whereas one who has been dishonoured will
be scorned and of little account. The ancestors can also be
brought back into the world physically during the *egungun*
rituals. *Egungun* masks cover the entire body. They are kept
secretly and worn by selected men of the community in
ceremonies in which it is held that the masks actually become
manifestations of the ancestors.

Beyond the world of men, the Yoruba world view includes
a pantheon of deities whom Soyinka himself has often equated
in at least some ways with the gods of ancient Greek
tradition. These gods are not infallible or immutable. Instead
they have different aspects to their being. Hence, Ogun,
Soyinka's favourite god, is the god of creation and in another
aspect he is also the god of destruction who, in a drunken
rage, once carried out a dreadful massacre. There are a few
major gods followed by a host of more minor deities. People
often choose one god in particular with whom they identify, to
whom they make regular offerings and from whom they seek

help. The gods can be approached through various mediums and priests or via offerings and rituals conducted by members of a community.

Essentially everything, according to Yoruba thought, is imbued with a spirit. Places and plant life may have spiritual significance. There are also spirits, both beneficent and malevolent, who can have an impact on the world of the living. In order to maintain the balance of harmony in an all-living world, man must be aware of the potential significance of any act. In particular, there are pre-eminent people, usually kings, chiefs or spiritual leaders, who are responsible for maintaining the balance of the world on behalf of the community and who must be prepared to go to considerable lengths, even death, in order to serve their people.

Wole Soyinka and Nigeria

Wole Soyinka was born in 1934, the son of a canon of the Anglican church. Although his parents were Christian, many of his relations followed traditional Yoruba beliefs. In a lyrical book of childhood reminiscences, *Aké: The Years of Childhood*, Soyinka shows how both sides of his inheritance had a formative influence on the writer-to-be.

Later Soyinka went to Ibadan University before studying English at Leeds University in 1956. From 1957 to 1959 Soyinka worked as a playreader for London's Royal Court Theatre. He also started to experiment with writing his own plays. In 1960 Soyinka returned to Nigeria and formed a new theatre company, The 1960 Masks. This group performed the playwright's first major work, *A Dance of the Forests*, which was commissioned for the occasion of Nigerian Independence, also in 1960. It had been assumed that this would be an up-beat celebratory piece, but Soyinka chose to be politically contentious even at this juncture, writing a play which took a sharply questioning look at Nigeria's pre-colonial history.

In the early 1960s Wole Soyinka was a prolific writer. He wrote not only plays but also his first novel, *The Interpreters*, and a volume of poetry, *Iandre and Other Poems*. All his major

themes are present in the early works. He is strongly critical
of politicians and fraudulent religious leaders, often using satire
to make his work more biting. He is interested in outstanding
individuals, their qualities and their duties. He is concerned
with the role of the artist in society. He is also concerned to
present his Yoruba-inspired vision of creation, where the
unborn, the living and the ancestors co-inhabit the world
along with the gods and spirits in a responsive harmony,
where all actions redound on all life and where there is no
essential division between the spiritual, the political and the
personal because all life partakes of the same sacred space.

In 1965 Soyinka's political involvements led to his arrest
after he seized a radio station and made a broadcast
questioning the veracity of the results of recent elections. The
playwright was acquitted within a couple of months, but in
1967, as Nigeria entered civil war, he was detained without
trial and held prisoner for over two years. His memories of
that time were later published as *The Man Died*. Soyinka then
produced a series of works in different genres: the poems
published as *A Shuttle in the Crypt*, the play *Madmen and
Specialists*, and the novel *Season of Anomy*, which explore the
debasing effects on entire peoples of corrupt leadership and
which scarify political tyranny.

From 1969 to 1976 Soyinka went into exile in Ghana and
Britain. During this time he edited a cultural and political
journal, *Transition*, later renamed *Ch'Indaba*. He published a
series of essays, *Myth, Literature and the African World* and he
wrote his most famous play, *Death and the King's Horseman*. Both
these two latter works explore the link between mythology and
performance. The masquerade of the *egungun* ritual is seen as
particularly significant in relation to African theatre, and the
role of the god Ogun as a central figure in Soyinka's
theatrical and moral consciousness is developed.

Death and the King's Horseman was directed by the playwright
on his return to Ife in Nigeria in 1976. He also set up the
Guerrilla Theatre Unit based at the University of Ife. In
contrast to Soyinka's work for the formal stage this group
mounted short plays and sketches in open-air public places,

although the targets remained corruption and government oppression. In the late seventies and the eighties Soyinka broadened the range of his political attack beyond Nigeria. The 1977 *Opera Wonyosi* was an attack on abuse of power, which featured Bokassa, the dictator of the Central African Empire, while *A Play of Giants* (1985) focused on the atrocities committed by tyrants such as Uganda's Idi Amin and castigated the weakness of the international community in tackling such people.

Wole Soyinka has continued to combine art and politics. In the late 1980s up until 1993, he worked as Chairman of the Road Safety Corps, trying to address the problem of Nigeria's enormous number of motoring fatalities. He has also continued to be a thorn in the flesh for Nigeria's various military and civilian regimes, constantly refusing to be silenced, although some of his work such as the 1985 film, *Blues for a Prodigal*, has been censored by the government.

In 1986 Soyinka's international status was confirmed when he won Africa's first Nobel Prize for Literature. He is now commonly acknowledged to be Africa's foremost dramatist. The playwright's most recent work, *The Beatification of Area Boy*, could not be produced in Nigeria due to political oppression, but was instead premièred in Britain in 1995 at the West Yorkshire Playhouse in Leeds. The illegal government of General Abacha, with its increasing intolerance of opposition, forced Soyinka to flee Nigeria in 1996. In 1997 the government indicted him for treason and Soyinka became a political exile once more, travelling the world agitating for international action against the atrocities of the Abacha regime.

The impact of Soyinka

Soyinka's influence in both artistic and political spheres has been enormous. He has been a role model to Africans, particularly in Nigeria but also in other parts of the continent. He has demonstrated over and over again that African theatre can be a powerful and aesthetic tool, giving Africans an artistic and philosophical voice in the world. His work spans almost the entire post-colonial period, and he has seen modern African theatre develop from a series of tentative experiments to a force which has many manifestations and an increasingly strong voice, which engages a huge number of people continent-wide in making theatre for and about African peoples. Though it is impossible to measure, Soyinka's uncompromising moral and political stands may well have strengthened other writers' resolve in refusing to be silenced by oppressive regimes throughout the continent.

Wole Soyinka's work is not, however, unquestioned. He has often been criticised as an élitist. There are a number of reasons for this. Firstly, he writes in English, a language only accessible to the educated minority of Africans and to foreign audiences. Secondly, his plays can be difficult. Soyinka's writing is always complex both linguistically and in the development of the philosophy of his plays. He resists simple black and white portrayals of characters and situations because this is not the way he sees the world. He expects an audience to do more than receive his plays passively and refuses to simplify his work in order to make life easy for his audiences. Thirdly, a number of critics object to Soyinka's concern for the exceptional individual. This has been the case particularly among more Marxist critics who claim that the playwright overvalues the impact of 'great men' at the expense of recognising the role of the mass of the people.

Soyinka has also been taken to task by a number of African critics for being too influenced by Western theatrical models in his acknowledged borrowings from, for instance, Shakespeare and the Greeks, and even in writing for the formal theatre when there are relatively few suitable auditoria for his plays in Africa. At the other end of the spectrum he has been accused of being too insular, writing from a complex Yoruba understanding of the world which makes his plays inaccessible and even irrelevant to outsiders.

Avowedly socialist writers such as Femi Osofisan have disputed with Soyinka over his use of Yoruba mythology in his plays. Osofisan complains that Soyinka simply accepts much Yoruba philosophy in a way that is potentially reactionary, rather than critically re-evaluating his inheritance in order to weigh up the influence of traditional mythology in the present day. Finally, many feminists question Soyinka's representation of women in his work. They complain that the female characters are stereotypical and symbolic rather than rounded portrayals of real women. They also point out that women are often objects rather than subjects, serving as virgins, mothers, whores or witches in order to tell us something about the male protagonists rather than anything about the women themselves.

Soyinka has vigorously defended his writing in books such as *Myth, Literature and the African World* and the more recent *Art, Dialogue and Outrage*. The measure of the controversy he has aroused is indicative of his stature in the world of African letters. He has been more written about than any other African writer. Indeed he has complained that there are too many critics of his work who might be better employed trying to produce creative work of their own.

In the political sphere Soyinka has been no less controversial. Most obviously, a series of Nigerian leaders have resented his intrusions into the world of politics and have tried in various ways to silence his voice. However, Soyinka is only one of a large number of politically outspoken writers, both in Nigeria and in Africa as a whole. He has refused to be silenced, and it is important to realise that in many African countries writers have a far greater political impact than they do in the West: they have often been leading figures in resisting totalitarian regimes. Quite simply, in Africa, theatre and literature still matter. Soyinka has often lent his powerful voice to the defence of other literary figures: recently in his unsuccessful campaign to save the life of Ken Saro-Wiwa, a popular Nigerian writer and leader of the Ogoni peoples in their attempt to gain recompense for the poisoning of their land by oil companies. Soyinka does not see how politics can be separated from art since both are part of life, and he resists calls for the separation of political action from artistic life. As he demonstrates in his play *Kongi's Harvest*, he knows very well that resistance to political tyranny may fail and even lead to death, but he does not see that as an excuse for not confronting the forces of evil.

Nigeria has been in the forefront of African post-colonial writing in general and theatre in particular: partly because it has such rich indigenous performance traditions, but also because it has had a relatively well-developed education sector and sufficient wealth – largely as a result of the oil boom of the 1970s – to fund publication and the provision of theatre facilities and training. Wole Soyinka is passionately engaged with Nigeria, as, like many African writers, he struggles with issues of nationalism and the question of how to resist oppressive government. Soyinka is first and foremost a Yoruba and a Nigerian, but he is also an international voice, for the issues he raises are not unique to his homeland but carry resonances for all concerned with the state of mankind and the joy of art.

Commentary

The history of the play

Death and the King's Horseman draws its seed from a real event that happened in Nigeria in 1945.

The Alafin (King) of Oyo, Oba Siyenbola Oladigbolu 1, died after a thirty-three-year reign. His 'Horseman', Olokun Esin Jinadu, had led a traditionally privileged life and the people of Oyo expected that he would carry out his duty and 'follow his master' by a ritual suicide. When the Alafin died the Horseman was delivering a message in the village of Ikoyi. About three weeks later he returned to Oyo, dressed himself in white and, in a traditional build-up to committing suicide, began dancing through the streets. The British colonial officer in charge at Oyo heard of Olokun Esin's intention and ordered that the Horseman should be prevented from killing himself. When word of his father's arrest reached the Horseman's youngest son, Murana, he killed himself in place of Olokun Esin in order to fulfil the needs of the ritual.

This story was told to Wole Soyinka in 1960 by Ulli Beier, and it stayed at the back of his mind until one day in 1974, when he was at Churchill College, Cambridge, and the play was 'triggered' when he walked past a bust of Winston Churchill. It was written very fast and given a first reading in Cambridge before being performed in Nigeria on his return home.

The rewriting of African myth and history in dramatic form has been common for many modern African writers as they seek to find 'truths' often suppressed or ignored in colonial or post-independence versions of African history. Soyinka has freely reinterpreted the story, while keeping close to its major events, in order to explore his ideas on leadership, tradition and the gulf between peoples.

The characters

Elesin

Elesin is the King's Horseman. This title carries with it
considerable honour which enables its holder to live as a great
chief. Elesin has been the King's close friend and adviser,
given all the worldly goods he could desire, and has enjoyed
the love of many women. The title, which is hereditary, also
carries with it one great duty: thirty days after the King's
death, at the time of his burial, the Horseman must enter a
trance and willingly and wilfully die, in order to lead his
master through the dangerous passage between the world of
the living and that of the ancestors. By wilfully encountering
death in full knowledge of what he does, the Horseman
effectively nullifies the power of death over his people and
maintains the link between different states of being essential
for the well-being of the Yoruba world.

The Elesin we meet is a man full of vitality and love of life.
He relishes all earthly pleasures, and it is typical of him that
he chooses to take his leave of the world in the market-place,
the centre of worldly goods, commerce and engagement.
Elesin is also full of self-confidence. He has had everything he
wanted in life and boasts that he alone has no fear of death.

Many commentators on *Death and the King's Horseman* have
pointed out Olunde's role as a mouthpiece for the playwright.
However, Elesin himself also represents Wole Soyinka in
significant ways. Like Soyinka, he has tremendous presence
and a great gift for words and story-telling, as exemplified in
the parable of the Not-I bird. Soyinka is fascinated by the
power of the human will, especially in significant individuals,
and believes that control of the will is central to man's ability
to order the world rightly. In Elesin we see a man who
thought he had control of his will but who finally did not.
This failure of his central duty because of personal weakness
destroys Elesin but it also imperils the whole world.

Through the character of Elesin, Soyinka examines whether
it is possible for a man who has been deeply involved in the
things of this world finally to cast them off and seek instead
the higher good of spiritual duty. The outcome of the play

seems to argue that at the very least such a balance is difficult to maintain, and that attachment to material pleasure is likely to corrupt the will and endanger society.

Elesin belongs to Yoruba life. He believes in all its values and duties, as well as in the privileges that accrue to himself as a significant player in this society. He wants nothing to do with the white man's colonial world. Hence his disowning his son when Olunde went to study in England. However, this attitude also means that Elesin has no understanding of, or defence against, intrusions from the colonial realm. He cannot deal with something he does not understand any more than Pilkings can deal with the Yoruba world.

Ultimately Elesin's love of women and life, as well as his hubris, come together – through the catalyst of Pilkings' attempt to stop the ritual suicide – to cause his will to fail on the very lip of the abyss between the worlds of the living and the ancestors. After his pride, his fall is immense. He is heaped with scorn by all who have loved him most and manacled by the white man like a slave from former times. Initially Elesin makes some weak attempts to defend himself, seeking to cast blame on Pilkings or on his young wife. But as a failed Horseman he knows he has lost all honour. From being the highest he has become the lowest. Only when he accepts that the failure is his alone does he regain some dignity. Finally, confronted by a despised son who has died in his father's place, Elesin knows that he cannot live on as an 'eater of left-overs'. He commits violent suicide. Not because this will put things right, for such a course is not possible now. Elesin will arrive amongst the ancestors too late, in dishonour. 'His son will feast on meat and throw him the bones. The passage is clogged with droppings from the King's stallion; he will arrive all stained in dung.' Elesin kills himself because he cannot bear to live with his shame and must at least attempt to atone for his betrayal of the community.

Elesin Oba is a hugely engaging character, but he is also a warning to the corrupt politicians Soyinka has written about so often. The corrupting dangers of power and prestige are

spelt out in unmistakable terms as Soyinka uses myth and
history to interrogate the contemporary world of Nigeria.

Iyaloja

Iyaloja is, in Soyinka's words, the 'Mother' of the market.
Market women in West Africa are powerful people. In many
West African towns and villages the market has been, and to
an extent still remains, the centre of earthly life and of
commerce. This trade is often controlled by women, the most
successful of whom may become enormously wealthy and
influential. As 'Mother' of the market we may presume that
Iyaloja is one of these wealthy, powerful women.

Like Elesin, Iyaloja is a traditionalist. She has little
knowledge of the colonial world and less use for it, as
evidenced in her scorn for the colonial police, and her
continual references to Pilkings as 'child'. She honours Elesin
as the upholder of the traditions and balance of the Yoruba
world, and she will therefore do anything for him which does
not transgress the rules of her world. However, this powerful
woman also knows Elesin well, and is not so much in awe of
him that she cannot speak freely. It is Iyaloja who warns
Elesin in Scene One not to be turned aside from his sacred
role by a lurking attachment to worldly things. She is, in
many ways, the nearest to an equal Elesin encounters. Both
are strong charismatic characters, who greatly enjoy each
other's company and wit. It is noteworthy that Elesin must
have Iyaloja's permission before he can claim his bride, who
has previously been betrothed to the market woman's son.

When Elesin fails in his ritual death it is Iyaloja's scorn he
must face, and Iyaloja who brings his son to the Horseman.
She is the upholder of Yoruba values, who in the final
moments of the play can order even Pilkings back from
interfering with Elesin's body and ensure that the bride, as the
vessel of future hope, carries out her prescribed role.

Iyaloja asserts her will, as matriarch, over the market
women, and by extension over a large part of the community.
Iyaloja knows and enjoys her power, but unlike Elesin she

never thinks she can transgress the fundamental rules which underpin the Yoruba world.

The Praise-Singer

Elesin's Praise-Singer is the most significant member of the Horseman's entourage. A great chief would always be surrounded by advisers and servants, and the Praise-Singer is one of these. The *griot* or praise-singer has an historic role in West African societies. He would often be entertainer, oral historian and story-teller as well as praise-singer, accompanying a great man and singing of his power and prowess.

The relationship between Elesin and his Praise-Singer is a close, even joking friendship for much of the early part of the play. They bandy jokes and proverbs. Both are consummate artists who revel in each other's talent. The Praise-Singer has a great love and admiration for Elesin. His final task for his master will be to help him reach the trance which will allow the Horseman to make the journey between this life and that of the ancestors, but he so loves and honours his master that the Praise-Singer would choose to accompany Elesin and sing his praises in the after-life as he has done on earth. Elesin affectionately jokes: 'You're like a jealous wife. Stay close to me, but only on this side.' The Praise-Singer has no independent life, he is given over to the service of his master, and after Elesin's projected triumphant death he intends to stay behind to continue singing the Horseman's praises. Like Iyaloja, the Praise-Singer also knows Elesin's weakness for earthly things, and he too dares to warn his master: 'Beware. The hands of women . . . weaken the unwary.'

In Scene Three it is the Praise-Singer who guides and facilitates Elesin's trance and his journey towards the passage between the states of being. His final oration is a wonderful recitative, helping us understand Elesin's journey, and expressing the Singer's great love for his master.

In the final scene the Praise-Singer's reproaches are added to Iyaloja's. But unlike Iyaloja the Praise-Singer speaks more in grief than in anger. He had offered to help Elesin on the way, but Elesin had been too proud and so has failed and upset the order of the world. The Praise-Singer speaks in the voice of a betrayed lover whose beloved has been found to have feet of clay.

Olunde

As Elesin's eldest son, Olunde should be the inheritor of the power and duties of the King's Horseman. As a member of the younger generation, like the market women's daughters, Olunde has come into more contact with the white colonials than the other major Nigerian characters, largely through his education. This was a common experience during the colonial period, when children might go to mission schools or government colleges which promoted white values and culture and often created a divorce in understanding between the older and younger generations.

Olunde is obviously an intelligent young man. In the past he dared create a rift with his father when he sought Pilkings' help to go to England and train as a doctor. Elesin and the Pilkings both think this means that Olunde has turned his back on the Yoruba world and accepted white values.

The immediate visual impression of Olunde conforms to such expectations as he is dressed in a European suit. However, we quickly learn that Olunde has returned in order to carry out his duties as eldest son after the death of his father. Olunde still honours his father and the traditional customs. He talks of Elesin's great will and confidently waits for the news of the ritual death. Contrary to the Pilkings' expectations, Olunde has not rejected Yoruba tradition. Instead he has used his time in Britain to further his understanding of the white races. That understanding does not reflect favourably on the whites – with a few honourable exceptions. Olunde is horrified by white hypocrisy and lies, and most of all by the arrogance which assumes that white people constitute a superior race, when they have, and seek to have, absolutely no understanding of the cultures and values of others.

Olunde, alone of all the characters in this play, understands both Yoruba and British societies. He is often seen as a mouthpiece for Soyinka's views. He has certainly made a similar journey to that of Soyinka, who was also educated in both Nigeria and England, and who is happy to make use of what he has learned from the white world, while remaining deeply Yoruba and inspired, as he says, by a Yoruba 'muse'. It is unfortunate that Olunde comes across as a slightly wooden prig, without the vibrant personality of the other characters in this play.

Finally, Olunde asserts his fundamental allegiances by taking his father's place, albeit without the proper ritual, as King's Horseman, and takes his own life in an effort to redress the dishonour and failure of his father. It is highly symbolic that Olunde is a doctor. He understands the ills of both societies and attempts to heal the sickness brought about by his father's failure by giving his own life instead.

Amusa

Sergeant Amusa is a 'Native Administration' policeman, that is, he is not employed by the British government but by the locally appointed leadership. This was the lowest form of police force in colonial Nigeria. Amusa is not Yoruba and is a Muslim. This is important in the play. Pilkings has thought that Amusa was 'better' than most Africans because he is not part of Yoruba, pagan society. However, Amusa is profoundly shocked by the Pilkings' wearing of *egungun* costumes as fancy dress. His sense of the sacred is outraged by this light treatment of the Yoruba religious masks and he refuses to talk to the Pilkings while they are dressed in such garb. The Pilkings see this behaviour as ridiculous, but Soyinka uses the scene to demonstrate Simon Pilkings' utter disregard for religious sensibilities.

Throughout the play Amusa is a source of light relief. We later meet him in the market-place when he attempts to arrest Elesin. He is no match for the wit of the market women and their daughters. As one who fully inhabits neither the Yoruba nor the white world, Amusa is generally seen as a white man's lackey who has sold his manhood to serve the colonists. He is therefore accorded little respect by either side.

Joseph

Joseph is the Pilkings' houseboy. African men were commonly referred to as 'boys' when they were household servants, no matter what their age. Unlike any of the other Yoruba people we meet, Joseph is a Christian convert. He has turned his back on Yoruba practices, but this does not mean Simon Pilkings accords him any more respect than any other African. Indeed he offends Joseph just as much as he does Amusa, but this time by casting scorn on Joseph's Catholic beliefs. Joseph has rather more dignity than Amusa and possibly more education, but he has also symbolically lost his manhood by accepting European rules and culture and becoming forever a 'boy'.

Simon Pilkings

As the British Distrist Officer, Pilkings is responsible for maintaining order throughout his district. He must decide what to do about Elesin's suicide, which is against the law. Pilkings is representative of a fairly common type of colonial and expatriate. He is utterly certain that British values are superior to anything else the world may have to offer, and he therefore has little interest in learning anything about Yoruba culture. Pilkings is shallow and conventional. Moreover he has little real understanding of his own culture. He mocks Christianity as freely as he does paganism or Islam, and his prime concern for much of the play is to impress the Prince at the fancy-dress ball by wearing and displaying his *egungun* costume. Pilkings learns nothing in the course of this play. His mind is utterly closed to new ideas. He might well be seen as a complete caricature were it not for the fact that many expatriates in Africa, even today, behave very similarly to Simon Pilkings.

Jane Pilkings

Jane is a rather more sympathetic version of her husband. She also wears the *egungun* costume with no compunction, and like her husband is vastly excited at the thought of meeting the Prince. However, she does try to curb her husband's wilder excesses of insensitivity. She urges compromise over upsetting Amusa's and Joseph's religious beliefs, and she listens, even if she learns very little, to Olunde's views on Yoruba and Western cultures. She is more sensible than her husband but is equally bound by a set of narrow values. She cannot even understand the significance of her own story about the captain who sacrificed himself for the greater good of society, and she is utterly shocked by Olunde's calm attitude to his father's intended sacrifice.

Themes

The significant individual

Wole Soyinka believes that certain people have special roles and duties in the world. This might apply to someone in any position, but it is particularly the case for those who are leaders of the people. Along with many other African writers, he has often emphasised the belief that leaders must be first and foremost servants of their people, and that ultimately their power and honour derive from the fact that they must be prepared to make great sacrifices for the community when necessary. This is a theme Soyinka has returned to in many of his plays, for instance in *Kongi's Harvest* and *The Strong Breed*.

Soyinka has been called élitist by a number of his contemporaries, partly because of this emphasis he puts on the influence of pre-eminent individuals. However he argues that history demonstrates how leaders can and have influenced major events, and in *Death and the King's Horseman* he explores what happens when a great leader fails in his duty to his people. In this case the failure of one man throws the future

of the whole of Yoruba society into doubt. Elesin's betrayal of
duty and trust is seen as catastrophic to his world.

Duty and will

Soyinka is a strong believer in duty. In *Death and the King's
Horseman* we see that those who follow their duty, such as the
bride and Olunde, maintain the harmonious balance of the
world. Our personal attitude to Elesin's ritual suicide is largely
irrelevant. The central point is that he has accepted a duty.
He has also accepted the honour and luxury that accrue to
him because the community knows the role he will ultimately
play as King's Horseman. When he fails to honour this
community trust and carry out a duty he has accepted, Elesin
falls lower than the lowest beggar and is rejected, first by his
son and later by others in Yoruba society. The betrayal of
trust and duty leads almost inevitably to tragedy and disaster,
and the more significant the individual the greater the
consequences of the betrayal.

Companion to the question of duty comes the question of
will. Once more this is an issue Soyinka has raised in a
number of his writings, including his prison book, *The Man
Died*. In that book Soyinka takes us through his own time as a
political prisoner when, in order to maintain his sense of
himself and his sanity, he gave himself tests of will. Frequently
he refused to eat, and even drank only minimally, in order to
assert his sense of will and control over himself and his
circumstances. He has also spoken eloquently, particularly in
the volume of essays, *Myth, Literature and the African World View*,
of how only the god Ogun dared to forge a link between the
world of the gods and the world of men, traversing a terrible
abyss by means of his will. For Soyinka it is the exercise of
will which makes us more than mere flotsam on the aimless
tides and currents of the human ocean, and it is only by
being in control of the will, absolutely, that man can control
his destiny.

In the case of Elesin, the Horseman tries, at the beginning
of Scene Five, to cast the blame for his failure to die on a

number of causes. He thinks to blame his wife, claiming that
her sexual loveliness dragged him back. He also seeks to put
the blame on Simon Pilkings for interrupting his trance as it
neared the moment of climax. However, both Soyinka in his
preface and Elesin in the text state that the failure had
nothing to do with the forces of colonialism. Elesin was pulled
back by a failure of will. He had boasted that he was an
extraordinary man, but at the crucial moment his will was
weak and he could not carry out the duty which only a man
fully in control of himself would have been able to
accomplish.

Power and corruption – political metaphor
Absolute power corrupts absolutely. So goes the saying.
Elesin's power has not been absolute and he is not corrupted
absolutely in that he retains a conscience, and he had
certainly intended to carry out his duty until his own weakness
of will betrayed him. But, we have to examine what it was
that dragged Elesin back. In the first scene he is warned by
both Iyaloja and the Praise-Singer to beware of his weakness
for women. We also witness how attracted Elesin is by the
vitality of human life as symbolised by his love of the market-
place. Such a hedonistic love of life goes ill with the willed
rejection of earthly things required if Elesin is to make the
move across the transitional gulf to the world of the ancestors.
In *Death and the King's Horseman* Soyinka examines the
difficulties of reconciling hedonism and earthly power with the
resolve to serve one's community through conscious sacrifice.

Moreover Elesin has become used to the honour in which
he is held by the people and this has led to his hubristic
claims that he is greater than other men, that he has no fear
of death or doubt that he will be able to carry out his self-
sacrificial duty. Hubris is another danger inherent in the
possession of earthly power. The flattery, honour and love of
the people has made Elesin over-confident in his own abilities
and he rejects the help offered by the Praise-Singer.

Soyinka has long been interested in the way leaders are so

often corrupted by power. Because Nigeria has had such a troubled recent history – with civilian governments constantly being overthrown by military coups and the huge trauma of the Nigerian Civil War in the 1960s – many Nigerian writers have used their talents to interrogate the ruling classes, to criticise abuses of power and to take committed political positions. Soyinka has been at the forefront of this politically engaged writing. Through the character of Elesin he examines how a man's good intentions may be corrupted when he has access to many earthly goods and to earthly power. Like many of Soyinka's plays, *Death and the King's Horseman* may also be read as a political parable in which the playwright is warning leaders, both spiritual and political, to beware of losing their way, of forgetting their primary function as servants of the community and being seduced by the attractions of wealth, lust and power.

Spirituality and politics

In the West we have become accustomed to writers being categorised by narrow definitions such as political, romantic, religious, historical, etc. It is important to realise that such definitions reflect the dominant rationalism of European thought from the eighteenth century onwards and a tendency in monotheistic religions such as Islam and Christianity to view life in dualistic terms: something is either good or evil, rational or emotional, political or religious. The more inclusive African world view tends not to see life in exclusive terms. Instead, all aspects of life are seen as related to each other, and an event taking place in an emotional sphere may well impact on political and/or spiritual life.

Death and the King's Horseman is a tale which relates not just to one aspect of life, but which sees the political and the spiritual as intimately entwined. Body, mind and soul are given equal priority in this play. The personal is political; the political is spiritual; and the spiritual affects both the individual and the entire world. Western criticism tends not to give weight equally to rational and mystical experience.

Soyinka demands that we see how all aspects of life are related across these different areas of sensibility. The responsibility for taking or not taking any action is heightened when we bring such an awareness to bear. We see how Elesin's failure to act appropriately is not simply failure for or by an individual. According to the script, it is not even failure for or by a community, it is an act which may potentially affect the entire world and even the world of the ancestors, rocking the spiritual and the political basis of the world.

Reclaiming history and culture

During the colonial period white missionaries, administrators, traders and settlers all conspired, like Simon Pilkings, to ridicule and devalue indigenous African cultures. The official stance was that Africa had no culture prior to the coming of the white man, and that it was the duty of the colonists to 'civilise' black people, to convert them to Christianity and to educate them in white values. All this was actually a means of justifying the inhuman exploitation of Africa, first through the slave trade and later by robbing the people of their land and resources in order to benefit European industry and empire.

Regrettably many colonists, like the Pilkings, accepted the justifying propaganda at face value. This meant they had no interest in, or respect for, indigenous cultures. In many parts of the British Empire indigenous religions and cultural forms of expression were suppressed. Missionaries opened schools in order to christianise an élite group of people. They also wished to create a local leadership which would be inculcated with Western values. This has led to considerable divisions between westernised and other Africans, with some educated Africans so thoroughly absorbing Western propaganda that they became ashamed of their indigenous forms of religion, marriage, music, dress, etc.

In the post-independence period in Africa, which for most countries happened in the 1960s, we see a spate of novels, poems and plays, which seek to revalue African cultures and to question the values imposed by colonialism. Some of these

were uncritically approving of all things African and damning
of the West. This has never been Soyinka's line. He is
extremely critical of colonialism, as demonstrated in the
portrayal of the whites and the satirical exchange amongst the
market girls. In contrast he gives us a Yoruba world which is
rich and vibrant, but it is not an uncritical portrait. Ritual
death is not the simplest topic to tackle if one seeks uncritical
approval of indigenous African cultures. Moreover, one of the
reasons for Elesin's failure is that he does not understand the
colonial world any more than the Pilkings understand him. He
is therefore vulnerable to attack from that world.

In the character of Olunde, Wole Soyinka argues that in
the contemporary world only mutual understanding of cultures
will prove fruitful. Neither the Pilkings nor Elesin and his
followers can learn from the alien cultures they encounter
because they are too certain of their own absolute rightness
and superiority; their closed minds prevent them seeing either
their own or any other culture objectively. Olunde has dared
cause a major rift with his father in order to travel to Europe
and gain an understanding of the colonial race on their own
home ground. Elesin thought this meant a rejection of the old
ways in favour of British culture – as did the whites – but
Olunde has used his time to learn a useful skill, doctoring,
and to analyse white society. The results of his understanding
are largely damning of the white world, but because he
understands their culture while they do not understand his,
Olunde has an advantage which enables him to triumph over
the will of the white world as represented by the Pilkings.

Soyinka has always advocated learning from other cultures,
and using whatever knowledge may be useful. The point is
not to learn uncritically, and not to forget or scorn, even
though one may criticise, the culture from which one
originates.

Language

Wole Soyinka is a poet, polemicist, essayist and novelist as
well as a playwright. He is acutely aware of the power and

tone of language which he uses as an immensely flexible tool.

One of the major points of contention among post-colonial African writers of all kinds has been just what language they should use. Because of the circumstances of European colonialism nearly all educated Africans have fluent command of not only one or more than one indigenous language but also of a European tongue: English, French or Portuguese, according to who colonised the nations concerned. Many writers take the position that they should write in an indigenous language in order to communicate with as many of the ordinary people as possible. However, such a position normally excludes the wider public, certainly at an international level but also, often, domestically, as many countries in Africa have a large number of indigenous languages. The debate remains unresolved, not least because conditions and the status of various languages vary widely from country to country. In Nigeria there are many people who write in indigenous tongues, but a substantial number of renowned writers have chosen, like Soyinka, to use English.

A problem for many such writers has been how to make English reflect the cadences and patterns of African speech. In *Death and the King's Horseman* we can see how Soyinka has dealt with this problem by using several different kinds of speech. The traditional Yoruba people use a weighty poetic language, rich in the proverbs and sayings which are intrinsic to many African languages. In heightened moments such as Elesin's recital of the Not-I bird story or the exchange between the Praise-Singer and Elesin leading into the trance, Soyinka moves into a speech pattern which is even more obviously poetic to reflect the nature of these passages.

In contrast, the language of the colonials is a thin, slangy form of English which lacks the rootedness shown in every utterance of Elesin and Iyaloja, who continually refer to the worlds of myth, history and story-telling. Soyinka's acute awareness of the significance of different patterns of speech is most clearly demonstrated in the exchange in Scene Three between the girls and the police. The girls parody European manners and speech and in so doing not only mock Sergeant

Amusa but also expose the stereotypical nature of many colonial encounters.

Amusa speaks yet another form of English. His is the English of the common man in Nigeria, a pidgin which has almost attained the status of an entirely distinct language. Here Soyinka uses a simplified form of pidgin so that standard English speakers will be able to understand the Sergeant, but his use of this form very definitely separates Amusa from the other characters in the play and emphasises his comic status.

We must not forget that the Yoruba language itself is embedded deeply in this play. Numerous Yoruba words are used as well as occasional whole lines. Moreover all the songs of the women are given in Yoruba, so that the sense of this land and its voice fill the play.

In *Death and the King's Horseman* the literary text is, however, only one of the chosen languages. Soyinka himself says that '*Death and the King's Horseman* can be fully realised only through an evocation of music from the abyss of transition.' If we look carefully at the stage directions we become aware that music of some kind is almost always present in the play, deepening and enriching our understanding and experience of this world. The drums are constantly in the background, both speaking and playing. There are also the songs of the market women, which move from the celebratory to a dirge as the tragedy of the play deepens. Music and drumming are essential to the journey Elesin makes towards the land of the ancestors as he enters his trance; while the dirge of the women is the background, unwavering, throughout the whole of the last half of the tragedy of Scene Five.

As in the written language, Soyinka contrasts Western music with Yoruba musicality greatly to the disadvantage of the former. Pilkings is first discovered to a background not of live or even English music, but with a tango playing on an old gramophone. In Scene Four Soyinka makes a point of telling us that the band (of local police) play 'Rule Britannia' badly before moving into a Viennese waltz. The colonials are cut off from their own culture and their music is merely tawdry and second-rate.

Soyinka writes of the 'threnodic essence' of this play and, even more than in most of his work, music speaks throughout *Death and the King's Horseman* as loudly and as powerfully as any words. In the talking drums the forms of language literally merge, communicating across the spectrum of emotional, spiritual and rational understanding.

Production history of *Death and the King's Horseman*

December 1976	World première, directed by Soyinka himself at the University of Ife.
October 1979	Second production, directed by Soyinka, at the Goodman Theater, Chicago. It transfers to the Kennedy Center, Washington DC, for a three-week season.
March 1987	Third production, again directed by Soyinka, at the Vivian Beaumont Theater at the Lincoln Center, New York.
22 November 1990	First British professional production opens at Royal Exchange Theatre, Manchester, directed by Phyllida Lloyd.
17 September 1995	First broadcast of BBC Radio production directed by Alby James.

An interview with Wole Soyinka

This is an edited version of an interview which was carried out in association with BBC Radio for the radio version of the play directed by Alby James in 1995.

Alby   Wole Soyinka, *Death and the King's Horseman* was written when you were a Fellow at Churchill College, Cambridge, in the mid-seventies. From where or what did the idea of the play come?

Soyinka   Well, the story of the play was actually brought to my attention by Ulli Beier many, many years before then in the early sixties. He was very taken with this story, this truthful bit of history which he'd collected, and it stuck in my head somewhere, as is usual with these things, but didn't resurface until I was in Churchill College. I was walking up or down the stairs one day at Churchill College – named after Winston Churchill – and the bust of this very bulldog Britisher was at the top of the stairs. And I saw this face, this representation of the colonial experience on society and the story came back. A few days later I found myself writing it almost compulsively. Obviously it had been gestating for quite a while somewhere in my subconscious and it only required that triggering figure, sitting on the plinth, to remind me of the story, to remind me of the strange byways our history has taken as a result – partly sometimes or, more crucially, totally – of the colonial intrusion.

Alby   So even in its creation, the idea of juxtaposing the two cultures, the English and the African, was part of its original formulation. Let's just explore that a bit further. The play sets death very much at the centre of the story. Elesin Oba wants to commit a redemptive suicide on behalf of his community and the British administration official can only see his death as an individual act, as an act of suicide, which he feels he has to stop. Is that how/where the clash of cultures in the play occurs?

Soyinka   Well, in fact, the moment you started speaking I wanted to pick on this word 'juxtaposition'. Juxtaposition of the colonial culture and the traditional experience of peoples. You see, for any kind of drama, any kind of dramatic event, what we term dramatic event – that is, something that moves slightly out of the ordinary – there is always a circumstance that triggers off that abnormality, that creates drama-worthy attention. In this case it was, indeed, the colonial set of values, but I always insist that this kind of tragedy could have taken place without external intrusion.

We have, for instance, a similar story of an Oba who wanted to perpetuate his line of succession and this was resisted by the chiefs who said, without the help of any kind of colonial intrusion, 'Listen! No! In our tradition we do not serve the father and serve the son.' And this led to devastating wars in Yorubaland in Nigeria.

So I don't like the play to be seen as one of a clash of cultures, because we do have both tragic drama and comic drama resulting from within the internal factors in society, [factors] which go to make up a tradition, a culture, a history.

Alby   Indeed, and in your introduction to the published version of the play you are careful to, let's say, 'admonish' any potential director to avoid the familiar, what you call 'reductionist tendency' of approaching the play as a conventional 'clash of cultures play' and to take care to direct his or her vision to the more difficult task, as you call it, of eliciting the play's 'threnodic' or lament quality/purpose. Does this suggest that you see the play's message as ultimately one of achieving a nemesis and if so, are you communicating your sense of hopelessness in the face of an unrelenting modernisation and Westernisation of African societies, potentially leading to the destruction of fundamental tribal values?

Soyinka   Well, two issues are sort of elicited out of this play. One, of course, is the whole concept of death. What does death mean in different societies? The death of an individual, the death of an ideal, the death of society itself through a failure of another value which we can call honour: a sense of honour, settlement of debts. The Yoruba world view, as you know, is one which accepts the continuity of the world of the living, the world of the ancestor and the world of the unborn. This, of course, reduces the kind of finality which death has for certain other societies.

There is also the question of honour. A society loses its direction when it abandons the whole notion of there being a concept called honour, the fulfilment of pledges. It doesn't matter whether it's gambling debts or the ultimate self-sacrificial debt in times of crisis. Or as part-and-parcel of the regeneration of the earth, of society, of community. However much one likes to argue about whether such a notion is antiquated or not, that's not the issue. It's a question of: you make a pledge, you settle it, you fulfil it or you do not.

So the incident of the intervention of the District Officer representing certain values is only one that brings out, brings to the surface, the possibility of there being even a tension within society. For an example you can look at the arguments between Elesin Oba when he's in jail and Pilkings. So it's not a statement of hopelessness in view of modernisation. No. I, for instance, depending on what mood I'm in, applaud Elesin Oba for accepting the intervention in his societal cause. Another time you may find me saying, 'Well, he made a pledge, he should have fulfilled it.' So I'm merely trying to have a dramatic exposition of a true story looking at it from both sides. Doing my best with my bias to give equal weight to both arguments.

Alby   So the play has multiple meanings. Could I also say, therefore, that something else quite clearly articulated by you in the play and intentionally so is that salvation of a society depends very much on an individual heroic act?

Soyinka   Well, I would not call the fulfilment of a pledge a heroic act. No. It's simply the termination of a certain course, a certain course of action. No, Elesin's act of ritual suicide in Yoruba tradition – and in certain other African traditions, by the way – I wouldn't call heroic. The man has had a very good time. He has lived like a king virtually. Anything which he desired was given to him or he took from people whether they were willing or not. And the understanding – the arrangement – was that when the time comes, he goes. There's nothing heroic about that. No.

And the question of salvation of society depending on an individual heroic act. Well, that is the history of society: that certain acts – either symbolic or, indeed, physical or metaphysical – by individuals within society can change the course of history for a society for better or worse.

One example, contemporary. The action of one stubborn dictator in Nigeria has set the country called Nigeria tumbling down a precipice the end of which is not yet in sight. Now, if it had been a different kind of person, for instance – and now I'm approaching it from the negative side – if it had been a very different kind of person, if he had taken a certain action at a crucial moment, that individual, by name I. B. Babangida, probably would be riding around the whole country on a white horse in robes of gold.

Alby   It seems to me that you're suggesting that this play is saying that countries like Nigeria suffer from failure of leadership?

Soyinka   Very much so. You see, historians like to be very tidy. They like to be schematic and this is especially so from, as you know, Marxist history, which tries to suggest almost a kind of mathematical unrolling of a social equation leading to a utopia within society. When people write history – most historians – they tend to sort of tidy up events in such a way as to eliminate the very crucial factor of the human element. Now I don't accept that. I look at the history of many, many societies and I think that those who are interested in the psychology of power as I am can see very often that the histories of certain societies have, in fact, been turned this way or that way because of the psychological make-up of certain individuals. Now it's a fact which I find is terribly neglected in historicism and I think this is where writers, those who reconstruct facts, try to compensate for this neglected aspect of history.

Alby   So you're trying to get the people to be aware of . . . let's call it the enemy within?

Soyinka   The enemy within, very much so. To balance the negative one I've just cited, look at South Africa and Mandela.

The history of South Africa today can be understood in a large part by the very strange chemistry between Mandela and de Klerk which developed, of course, over time and in the very unique personality of Nelson Mandela. The history of South Africa as it is today cannot neglect that human factor. So societies have got to be extremely careful about who they acknowledge and encourage as their leaders. That's why I happen to believe in democracy, because it gives the people a chance at least to question, to choose and to try and change whenever necessary the quality, the person or the group – the clique if you like – whatever it is, which represents leadership within a society.

Alby   Well, let's see how this links into the wider issues of what being a Yoruba means. In the play *Death and the King's Horseman* the character you call the Mother of the Market, Iyaloja, commands Elesin to recognise that he holds within him the potential to sacrifice, to threaten these great traditions of the Yoruba people. You are fascinated by this whole Yoruba culture and the myths and legends within it, aren't you?

Soyinka   My muse happens to be the Yoruba world view.

Alby   What is, exactly, this tradition? Let us talk about the god Ogun.

Soyinka   Well, I think the Yoruba gods are so truthful. Truthful in the sense that I consider religion and the construct of deities simply an extension of human qualities taken, if you like, to the nth degree. I mistrust gods who become so separated from humanity that enormous crimes can be committed in their names. I prefer gods who can be brought down to earth and judged, if you like. And the Yoruba theogony very much embraces that world view. All the gods have their errors, their moment of error. The ills of the world are blamed on the deities but not in the absolute way of their knowing what they were doing at the time. They were either drunk when they did it, when they committed certain errors which were responsible for the creation of the cripples, etc. of the world or they were enfeebled in some other way. But more important is what I call the elasticity of the digestive system of the deities. Ogun is not a static deity.

Ogun embraces every new experience. Ogun is not just a neolithic kind of deity. The moment technology comes into the purlieu of the Yoruba, a deity is immediately found. In this case it's Ogun. In the case of electricity it's Shango. And as experience of the Yoruba world expands so do the deities. If you like, the Cabinet responsibilities of the deities are extended to embrace the new experiences.

There's something else which I never tire of saying. Yoruba religion, world view, is so self-confident that their adherents never proselytise. Never. And yet, in spite of this, the religion has survived across the waters. It exists in Haiti, Brazil, Cuba, Columbia, in several parts of Latin America, without any fuss. The Yoruba have never fought any war, neither *Jihad* or crusade, on behalf of their religion. Now this is a lesson which these very arrogant and mutually self-destructive religions – Christianity, Islam, Judaism, plus others like Hinduism – these belligerent, mutually murderous so-called world religions – had better learn from Yoruba religion. You will not find an adherent of a Yoruba deity going out to murder another being simply because that individual does not accept the tenets of his or her religion. I think in the present mutually self-destructive condition of the world, Yoruba religion is one religion in which other religious followers might learn a lesson in humility.

Alby   How does Ogun relate to your creative muse? I know he's the god of metallurgy or steel.

Soyinka   Yes, metallurgy. You know Ogun drew me very early to a recognition of himself as, if you like, my companion *d'energie*. First of all, he's a god of the lyric, the *ijala*. Through being the god of the lyric, the poetry of hunters, he is also the god of hunters. And again, through the fact that he is a god of metallurgy he's a god of those who work in metals, which includes hunters. So today Ogun is a god of railway workers, motor-car drivers and, unquestionably, of astronauts. We still wait to boast one from African society, but that will come. He, therefore, also represents both the destructive and creative principles which, whether we like it or not, is very much the ideogram of the world we live in.

Alby   So we have to treat him with care?

Soyinka   We have to treat him with care. We have to try constantly to attempt to make the pacific aspect of Ogun work for us because Ogun is also a lover of solitude. He's always going into retreat in the mountains, always expiating the errors which led him to destroy even his own people in the famous Battle of Ire when he came down among humanity, and so on. So you have to be very careful of this deity.

Alby   Wole Soyinka, thank you very much.

Further reading

By Wole Soyinka

Plays:
The Bacchae of Euripides (Methuen, 1973)
The Beatification of Area Boy (Methuen, 1995)
Camwood on the Leaves (Methuen, 1973)
A Dance of the Forests (Oxford University Press, 1963)
From Zia, With Love and A Scourge of Hyacinths (Methuen, 1992)
The Jero Plays: The Trials of Brother Jero and Jero's Metamorphosis
    (Methuen, 1973)
King Baabu (Methuen, 2002)
Kongi's Harvest (Oxford University Press, 1967)
The Lion and the Jewel (Oxford University Press, 1963)
Madmen and Specialists (Methuen, 1971)
Opera Wonyosi (Rex Collings, 1981; Methuen, 1984)
A Play of Giants (Methuen, 1984)
Requiem for a Futurologist (Rex Collings, 1985)
The Road (Oxford University Press, 1965)
The Strong Breed (in *Three Short Plays*, Oxford University Press, 1969)
The Swamp Dwellers (in *Three Short Plays*, Oxford University Press,
    1969)

Poetry:
Idanre and Other Poems (Methuen, 1967)
Ogun Abibiman (Rex Collings, 1976)
Mandela's Earth (André Deutsch, 1989; Methuen, 1990)
Samarkand and Other Markets I Have Known (Methuen, 2002)
A Shuttle in the Crypt (Methuen, 1972)

Fiction:
The Interpreters (André Deutsch, 1965)
Season of Anomy (Rex Collings, 1973)

Memoirs:
The Man Died (Prison Notes) (Rex Collings, 1972)
Aké: The Years of Childhood (Rex Collings, 1981; Minerva, 1991)
Ìsarà: A Voyage Around Essay (Methuen, 1990; Minerva, 1991)
Ibadan: The Penkelemes Years – A Memoir 1946–1965 (Methuen, 1994; Minerva, 1995)
You Must Set Forth At Dawn (Methuen, 2007)

Essays on art and culture:
Art, Dialogue and Outrage (Methuen, 1988)
Myth, Literature and the African World (Cambridge University Press, 1976)

Critical material

Dennis Duerden and Cosmo Pieterse, eds., *African Writers Talking* (London, Heinemann, 1972), pp. 169–80
James Gibbs, ed., *Critical Perspectives on Wole Soyinka* (London, Hutchinson, 1982)
Biodun Jeyifo, *Conversations with Wole Soyinka* (Mississippi, University Press of Mississippi, 2001)
Eldred Jones, *The Writing of Wole Soyinka* (London, Heinemann, 1981)
Adewale Maja-Pearce, *Wole Soyinka – An Appraisal* (London, Heinemann, 1986)
Gerald Moore, *Wole Soyinka* (London, Evans Brothers, 2nd edition 1978)
Oyin Ogunba, *The Movement of Transition: A Study of the Plays of Wole Soyinka* (Ibadan University Press, 1975)
Mark Ralph-Bowman, 'Leaders and Leftovers – A Reading of Soyinka's *Death and the King's Horseman*', *Research in African Literatures*, 14.1 (Austin, Texas, Spring 1983), pp. 81–97
Tejumola Olaniyan, *Scars of Conquest/Masks of Resistance: The Invention of Cultural Identities in African, African-American and Caribbean Drama* (Oxford University Press, 1995)

Death and the King's Horseman

Author's Note

This play is based on events which took place in Oyo, ancient Yoruba city of Nigeria, in 1946. That year, the lives of Elesin (Olori Elesin), his son, and the Colonial District Officer intertwined with the disastrous results set out in the play. The changes I have made are in matters of detail, sequence and of course characterisation. The action has also been set back two or three years to while the war was still on, for minor reasons of dramaturgy.

The factual account still exists in the archives of the British Colonial Administration. It has already inspired a fine play in Yoruba (*Oba Wàjà*) by Duro Ladipo. It has also misbegotten a film by some German television company.

The bane of themes of this genre is that they are no sooner employed creatively than they acquire the facile tag of 'clash of cultures', a prejudicial label which, quite apart from its frequent misapplication, presupposes a potential equality *in every given situation* of the alien culture and the indigenous, on the actual soil of the latter. (In the area of misapplication, the overseas prize for illiteracy and mental conditioning undoubtedly goes to the blurb-writer for the American edition of my novel *Season of Anomy* who unblushingly declares that this work portrays the 'clash between old values and new ways, between western methods and African traditions'!) It is thanks to this kind of perverse mentality that I find it necessary to caution the would-be producer of this play against a sadly familiar reductionist tendency, and to direct his vision instead to the far more difficult and risky task of eliciting the play's threnodic essence.

One of the more obvious alternative structures of the play would be to make the District Officer the victim of a cruel dilemma. This is not to my taste and it is not by chance that I have avoided dialogue or situation which would encourage this. No attempt should be made in production to suggest it. The Colonial Factor is an incident, a catalytic incident merely. The confrontation in the play is largely metaphysical, contained in the human vehicle which is Elesin and the universe of the Yoruba mind – the world of the living, the dead and the unborn, and the numinous passage which links all: transition. *Death and the King's Horseman* can be fully realised only through an evocation of music from the abyss of transition.

W.S.

Characters

Praise-Singer
Elesin, *Horseman of the King*
Iyaloja, *'Mother' of the market*
Simon Pilkings, *District Officer*
Jane Pilkings, *his wife*
Sergeant Amusa
Joseph, *houseboy to the Pilkings*
Bride
H.R.H. the Prince
The Resident
Aide-de-Camp
Olunde, *eldest son of Elesin*
Drummers, Women, Young Girls, Dancers at the Ball

The play should run without an interval. For rapid scene changes, one adjustable outline set is very appropriate.

Scene One

A passage through a market in its closing stages. The stalls are being emptied, mats folded. A few women pass through on their way home, loaded with baskets. On a cloth-stand, bolts of cloth are taken down, display pieces folded and piled on a tray. **Elesin Oba** *enters along a passage before the market, pursued by his drummers and praise-singers. He is a man of enormous vitality, speaks, dances and sings with that infectious enjoyment of life which accompanies all his actions.*

Praise-Singer   Elesin o! Elesin Oba! Howu! What tryst is this the cockerel goes to keep with such haste that he must leave his tail behind?

Elesin (*slows down a bit, laughing*)   A tryst where the cockerel needs no adornment.

Praise-Singer   O-oh, you hear that my companions? That's the way the world goes. Because the man approaches a brand-new bride he forgets the long faithful mother of his children.

Elesin   When the horse sniffs the stable does he not strain at the bridle? The market is the long-suffering home of my spirit and the women are packing up to go. That Esu-harassed day slipped into the stewpot while we feasted. We ate it up with the rest of the meat. I have neglected my women.

Praise-Singer   We know all that. Still it's no reason for shedding your tail on this day of all days. I know the women will cover you in damask and *alari* but when the wind blows cold from behind, that's when the fowl knows his true friends.

Elesin   Olohun-iyo!

Praise-Singer   Are you sure there will be one like me on the other side?

Elesin   Olohun-iyo!

Praise-Singer   Far be it for me to belittle the dwellers of that place but, a man is either born to his art or he isn't. And I don't know for certain that you'll meet my father, so who is

going to sing these deeds in accents that will pierce the
deafness of the ancient ones. I have prepared my going – just
tell me: Olohun-iyo, I need you on this journey and I shall be
behind you.

Elesin   You're like a jealous wife. Stay close to me, but only
on this side. My fame, my honour are legacies to the living,
stay behind and let the world sip its honey from your lips.

Praise-Singer   Your name will be like the sweet berry a
child places under his tongue to sweeten the passage of food.
The world will never spit it out.

Elesin   Come then. This market is my roost. When I come
among the women I am a chicken with a hundred mothers. I
become a monarch whose palace is built with tenderness and
beauty.

Praise-Singer   They love to spoil you but beware. The
hands of women also weaken the unwary.

Elesin   This night I'll lay my head upon their lap and go to
sleep. This night I'll touch feet with their feet in a dance that
is no longer of this earth. But the smell of their flesh, their
sweat, the smell of indigo on their cloth, this is the last air I
wish to breathe as I go to meet my great forebears.

Praise-Singer   In their time the world was never tilted from
its groove, it shall not be in yours.

Elesin   The gods have said No.

Praise-Singer   In their time the great wars came and went,
the little wars came and went; the white slavers came and
went, they took away the heart of our race, they bore away
the mind and muscle of our race. The city fell and was
rebuilt; the city fell and our people trudged through mountain
and forest to find a new home but – Elesin Oba do you hear
me?

Elesin   I hear your voice Olohun-iyo.

Praise-Singer   Our world was never wrenched from its true course.

Elesin The gods have said No.

Praise-Singer There is only one home to the life of a river-mussel; there is only one home to the life of a tortoise; there is only one shell to the soul of man; there is only one world to the spirit of our race. If that world leaves its course and smashes on boulders of the great void, whose world will give us shelter?

Elesin It did not in the time of my forebears, it shall not in mine.

Praise-Singer The cockerel must not be seen without his feathers.

Elesin Nor will the Not-I bird be much longer without his nest.

Praise-Singer (*stopped in his lyric stride*) The Not-I bird, Elesin?

Elesin I said, the Not-I bird.

Praise-Singer All respect to our elders but, is there really such a bird?

Elesin What! Could it be that he failed to knock on your door?

Praise-Singer (*smiling*) Elesin's riddles are not merely the nut in the kernel that breaks human teeth; he also buries the kernel in hot embers and dares a man's fingers to draw it out.

Elesin I am sure he called on you, Olohun-iyo. Did you hide in the loft and push out the servant to tell him you were out?

Elesin *executes a brief, half-taunting dance. The drummer moves in and draws a rhythm out of his steps.* **Elesin** *dances towards the market-place as he chants the story of the Not-I bird, his voice changing dexterously to mimic his characters. He performs like a born raconteur, infecting his retinue with his humour and energy. More* **Women** *arrive* *during his recital, including* **Iyaloja**.

Elesin
Death came calling
Who does not know his rasp of reeds?
A twilight whisper in the leaves before
The great araba falls? Did you hear it?
Not I! swears the farmer. He snaps
His fingers round his head, abandons
A hard-worn harvest and begins
A rapid dialogue with his legs.

'Not I,' shouts the fearless hunter, 'but –
It's getting dark, and this night-lamp
Has leaked out all its oil. I think
It's best to go home and resume my hunt
Another day.' But now he pauses, suddenly
Let's out a wail: 'Oh foolish mouth, calling
Down a curse on your own head! Your lamp
Has leaked out all its oil, has it?'
Forwards or backwards now he dare not move.
To search for leaves and make *etutu*
On that spot? Or race home to the safety
Of his hearth? Ten market-days have passed
My friends, and still he's rooted there
Rigid as the plinth of Orayan.

The mouth of the courtesan barely
Opened wide enough to take a ha'penny *robo*
When she wailed: 'Not I.' All dressed she was
To call upon my friend the Chief Tax Officer.
But now she sends her go-between instead:
'Tell him I'm ill: my period has come suddenly
But not – I hope – my time.'

Why is the pupil crying?
His hapless head was made to taste
The knuckles of my friend the Mallam:
'If you were then reciting the Koran
Would you have ears for idle noises

Darkening the trees, you child of ill omen?'
He shuts down school before its time
Runs home and rings himself with amulets.
And take my good kinsman Ifawomi.
His hands were like a carver's, strong
And true. I saw them
Tremble like wet wings of a fowl.
One day he cast his time-smoothed *opele*
Across the divination board. And all because
The suppliant looked him in the eye and asked,
'Did you hear that whisper in the leaves?'
'Not I,' was his reply; 'perhaps I'm growing deaf –
Good-day.' And Ifa spoke no more that day
The priest locked fast his doors,
Sealed up his leaking roof – but wait!
This sudden care was not for Fawomi
But for Osanyin, a courier-bird of Ifa's
Heart of wisdom. I did not know a kite
Was hovering in the sky
And Ifa now a twittering chicken in
The brood of Fawomi the Mother Hen.

Ah, but I must not forget my evening
Courier from the abundant palm, whose groan
Became Not I, as he constipated down
A wayside bush. He wonders if Elegbara
Has tricked his buttocks to discharge
Against a sacred grove. Hear him
Mutter spells to ward off penalties
For an abomination he did not intend.
If any here
Stumbles on a gourd of wine, fermenting
Near the road, and nearby hears a stream
Of spells issuing from a crouching form.
Brother to a *sigidi*, bring home my wine,
Tell my tapper I have ejected
Fear from home and farm. Assure him,
All is well.

Praise-Singer   In your time we do not doubt the peace of farmstead and home, the peace of road and hearth, we do not doubt the peace of the forest.

Elesin
There was fear in the forest too.
Not-I was lately heard even in the lair
Of beasts. The hyena cackled loud. Not I,
The civet twitched his fiery tail and glared:
Not I. Not-I became the answering-name
Of the restless bird, that little one
Whom Death found nesting in the leaves
When whisper of his coming ran
Before him on the wind. Not-I
Has long abandoned home. This same dawn
I heard him twitter in the gods' abode.
Ah, companions of this living world
What a thing this is, that even those
We call immortal
Should fear to die.

Iyaloja
But you, husband of multitudes?

Elesin
I, when that Not-I bird perched
Upon my roof, bade him seek his nest again.
Safe, without care or fear. I unrolled
My welcome mat for him to see. Not-I
Flew happily away, you'll hear his voice
No more in this lifetime – You all know
What I am.

Praise-Singer
That rock which turns its open lodes
Into the path of lightning. A gay
Thoroughbred whose stride disdains
To falter though an adder reared
Suddenly in his path.

Elesin

My rein is loosened.
I am master of my fate. When the hour comes
Watch me dance along the narrowing path
Glazed by the soles of my great precursors.
My soul is eager. I shall not turn aside.

Women

You will not delay?

Elesin

Where the storm pleases, and when, it directs
The giants of the forest. When friendship summons
Is when the true comrade goes.

Women

Nothing will hold you back?

Elesin

Nothing. What! Has no one told you yet
I go to keep my friend and master company.
Who says the mouth does not believe in
'No, I have chewed all that before?' I say I have.
The world is not a constant honey-pot.
Where I found little I made do with little.
Where there was plenty I gorged myself.
My master's hands and mine have always
Dipped together and, home or sacred feast,
The bowl was beaten bronze, the meats
So succulent our teeth accused us of neglect.
We shared the choicest of the season's
Harvest of yams. How my friend would read
Desire in my eyes before I knew the cause –
However rare, however precious, it was mine.

Women

The town, the very land was yours.

Elesin

The world was mine. Our joint hands
Raised houseposts of trust that withstood
The siege of envy and the termites of time.

But the twilight hour brings bats and rodents –
Shall I yield them cause to foul the rafters?

Praise-Singer
Elesin Oba! Are you not that man who
Looked out of doors that stormy day
The god of luck limped by, drenched
To the very lice that held
His rags together? You took pity upon
His sores and wished him fortune.
Fortune was footloose this dawn, he replied,
Till you trapped him in a heartfelt wish
That now returns to you. Elesin Oba!
I say you are that man who
Chanced upon the calabash of honour.
You thought it was palm wine and
Drained its contents to the final drop.

Elesin
Life has an end. A life that will outlive
Fame and friendship begs another name.
What elder takes his tongue to his plate,
Licks it clean of every crumb? He will encounter
Silence when he calls on children to fulfil
The smallest errand! Life is honour.
It ends when honour ends.

Women
We know you for a man of honour.

Elesin   Stop! Enough of that!

Women (*puzzled, they whisper among themselves, turning mostly to*
Iyaloja)   What is it? Did we say something to give offence?
Have we slighted him in some way?

Elesin   Enough of that sound I say. Let me hear no more in
that vein. I've heard enough.

Iyaloja   We must have said something wrong. (*Comes forward
a little.*) Elesin Oba, we ask forgiveness before you speak.

Elesin I am bitterly offended.

Iyaloja Our unworthiness has betrayed us. All we can do is ask your forgiveness. Correct us like a kind father.

Elesin This day of all days . . .

Iyaloja It does not bear thinking. If we offend you now we have mortified the gods. We offend heaven itself. Father of us all, tell us where we went astray. (*She kneels, the other* **Women** *follow.*)

Elesin
Are you not ashamed? Even a tear-veiled
Eye preserves its function of sight.
Because my mind was raised to horizons
Even the boldest man lowers his gaze
In thinking of, must my body here
Be taken for a vagrant's?

Iyaloja Horseman of the King, I am more baffled than ever.

Praise-Singer The strictest father unbends his brow when the child is penitent, Elesin. When time is short, we do not spend it prolonging the riddle. Their shoulders are bowed with the weight of fear lest they have marred your day beyond repair. Speak now in plain words and let us pursue the ailment to the home of remedies.

Elesin
Words are cheap. 'We know you for
A man of honour.' Well tell me, is this how
A man of honour should be seen?
Are these not the same clothes in which
I came among you a full half-hour ago?

He roars with laughter and the **Women**, *relieved, rise and rush into stalls to fetch rich clothes.*

Women The gods are kind. A fault soon remedied is soon forgiven. Elesin Oba, even as we match our words with deed, let your heart forgive us completely.

Elesin
>You who are breath and giver of my being
>How shall I dare refuse you forgiveness
>Even if the offence was real.

Iyaloja (*dancing round him. Sings*)
>He forgives us. He forgives us.
>What a fearful thing it is when
>The voyager sets forth
>But a curse remains behind.

Women
>For a while we truly feared
>Our hands had wrenched the world adrift
>In emptiness.

Iyaloja
>Richly, richly, robe him richly
>The cloth of honour is *alari*
>*Sanyan* is the band of friendship
>Boa-skin makes slippers of esteem.

Women
>For a while we truly feared
>Our hands had wrenched the world adrift
>In emptiness.

Praise-Singer
>He who must, must voyage forth
>The world will not roll backwards
>It is he who must, with one
>Great gesture overtake the world.

Women
>For a while we truly feared
>Our hands had wrenched the world
>In emptiness.

Praise-Singer
>The gourd you bear is not for shirking

The gourd is not for setting down
At the first crossroad or wayside grove
Only one river may know its contents.

Women

We shall all meet at the great market
We shall all meet at the great market
He who goes early takes the best bargains
But we shall meet, and resume our banter.

Elesin *stands resplendent in rich clothes, cap, shawl, etc. His sash is of a bright red alari cloth. The* **Women** *dance round him. Suddenly, his attention is caught by an object off-stage.*

Elesin

The world I know is good.

Women

We know you'll leave it so.

Elesin

The world I know is the bounty
Of hives after bees have swarmed.
No goodness teems with such open hands
Even in the dreams of deities.

Women

And we know you'll leave it so.

Elesin

I was born to keep it so. A hive
Is never known to wander. An anthill
Does not desert its roots. We cannot see
The still great womb of the world –
No man beholds his mother's womb –
Yet who denies it's there? Coiled
To the navel of the world is that
Endless cord that links us all
To the great origin. If I lose my way
The trailing cord will bring me to the roots.

Women
   The world is in your hands.

The earlier distraction, a beautiful young girl, comes along the passage through which **Elesin** *first made his entry.*

Elesin
   I embrace it. And let me tell you, women –
   I like this farewell that the world designed,
   Unless my eyes deceive me, unless
   We are already parted, the world and I,
   And all that breeds desire is lodged
   Among our tireless ancestors. Tell me friends,
   Am I still earthed in that beloved market
   Of my youth? Or could it be my will
   Has outleapt the conscious act and I have come
   Among the great departed?

Praise-Singer   Elesin Oba why do your eyes roll like a
bush-rat who sees his fate like his father's spirit, mirrored in
the eye of a snake? And all those questions! You're standing
on the same earth you've always stood upon. This voice you
hear is mine, Oluhun-iyo, not that of an acolyte in heaven.

Elesin
   How can that be? In all my life
   As Horseman of the King, the juiciest
   Fruit on every tree was mine. I saw,
   I touched, I wooed, rarely was the answer No.
   The honour of my place, the veneration I
   Received in the eye of man or woman
   Prospered my suit and
   Played havoc with my sleeping hours.
   And they tell me my eyes were a hawk
   In perpetual hunger. Split an iroko tree
   In two, hide a woman's beauty in its heartwood
   And seal it up again – Elesin, journeying by,
   Would make his camp beside that tree
   Of all the shades in the forest.

Praise-Singer   Who would deny your reputation, snake-on-
the-loose in dark passages of the market! Bed-bug who wages

war on the mat and receives the thanks of the vanquished!
When caught with his bride's own sister he protested – but I
was only prostrating myself to her as becomes a grateful in-
law. Hunter who carries his powder-horn on the hips and fires
crouching or standing! Warrior who never makes that excuse
of the whining coward – but how can I go to battle without
my trousers? – trouserless or shirtless it's all one to him. Oka-
rearing-from-a-camouflage-of-leaves, before he strikes the
victim is already prone! Once they told him, Howu, a stallion
does not feed on the grass beneath him: he replied, true, but
surely he can roll on it!

Women   Ba-a-a-ba O!

Praise-Singer   Ah, but listen yet. You know there is the
leaf-nibbling grub and there is the cola-chewing beetle; the
leaf-nibbling grub lives on the leaf, the cola-chewing beetle
lives in the colanut. Don't we know what our man feeds on
when we find him cocooned in a woman's wrapper?

Elesin
   Enough, enough, you all have cause
   To know me well. But, if you say this earth
   Is still the same as gave birth to those songs,
   Tell me who was that goddess through whose lips
   I saw the ivory pebbles of Oya's river-bed.
   Iyaloja, who is she? I saw her enter
   Your stall; all your daughters I know well.
   No, not even Ogun-of-the-farm toiling
   Dawn till dusk on his tuber patch
   Not even Ogun with the finest hoe he ever
   Forged at the anvil could have shaped
   That rise of buttocks, not though he had
   The richest earth between his fingers.
   Her wrapper was no disguise
   For thighs whose ripples shamed the river's
   Coils around the hills of Ilesi. Her eyes
   Were new-laid eggs glowing in the dark.
   Her skin . . .

Iyaloja   Elesin Oba . . .

Elesin   What! Where do you all say I am?

Iyaloja   Still among the living.

Elesin
And that radiance which so suddenly
Lit up this market I could boast
I knew so well?

Iyaloja   Has one step already in her husband's home. She is betrothed.

Elesin (*irritated*)   Why do you tell me that?

Iyaloja falls silent. The **Women** *shuffle uneasily.*

Iyaloja   Not because we dare give you offence Elesin. Today is your day and the whole world is yours. Still, even those who leave town to make a new dwelling elsewhere like to be remembered by what they leave behind.

Elesin
Who does not seek to be remembered?
Memory is Master of Death, the chink
In his armour of conceit. I shall leave
That which makes my going the sheerest
Dream of an afternoon. Should voyagers
Not travel light? Let the considerate traveller
Shed, of his excessive load, all
That may benefit the living.

Women (*relieved*)   Ah Elesin Oba, we knew you for a man of honour.

Elesin   Then honour me. I deserve a bed of honour to lie upon.

Iyaloja   The best is yours. We know you for a man of honour. You are not one who eats and leaves nothing on his plate for children. Did you not say it yourself? Not one who blights the happiness of others for a moment's pleasure.

Elesin
Who speaks of pleasure? O women, listen!
Pleasure palls. Our acts should have meaning.
The sap of the plantain never dries.
You have seen the young shoot swelling
Even as the parent stalk begins to wither.
Women, let my going be likened to
The twilight hour of the plantain.

Women What does he mean Iyaloja? This language is the
language of our elders, we do not fully grasp it.

Iyaloja I dare not understand you yet Elesin.

Elesin
All you who stand before the spirit that dares
The opening of the last door of passage,
Dare to rid my going of regrets! My wish
Transcends the blotting out of thought
In one mere moment's tremor of the senses.
Do me credit. And do me honour.
I am girded for the route beyond
Burdens of waste and longing.
Then let me travel light. Let
Seed that will not serve the stomach
On the way remain behind. Let it take root
In the earth of my choice, in this earth
I leave behind.

Iyaloja (*turns to* **Women**) The voice I hear is already
touched by the waiting fingers of our departed. I dare not
refuse.

Woman But Iyaloja . . .

Iyaloja The matter is no longer in our hands.

Woman But she is betrothed to your own son. Tell him.

Iyaloja My son's wish is mine. I did the asking for him, the
loss can be remedied. But who will remedy the blight of
closed hands on the day when all should be openness and

light? Tell him, you say! You wish that I burden him with knowledge that will sour his wish and lay regrets on the last moments of his mind. You pray to him who is your intercessor to the world – don't set this world adrift in your own time; would you rather it was my hand whose sacrilege wrenched it loose?

Woman Not many men will brave the curse of a dispossessed husband.

Iyaloja Only the curses of the departed are to be feared. The claims of one whose foot is on the threshold of their abode surpasses even the claims of blood. It is impiety even to place hindrances in their ways.

Elesin
What do my mothers say? Shall I step
Burdened into the unknown?

Iyaloja Not we, but the very earth says No. The sap in the plantain does not dry. Let grain that will not feed the voyager at his passage drop here and take root as he steps beyond this earth and us. Oh you who fill the home from hearth to threshold with the voices of children, you who now bestride the hidden gulf and pause to draw the right foot across and into the resting-home of the great forebears, it is good that your loins be drained into the earth we know, that your last strength be ploughed back into the womb that gave you being.

Praise-Singer Iyaloja, mother of multitudes in the teeming market of the world, how your wisdom transfigures you!

Iyaloja (*smiling broadly, completely reconciled*) Elesin, even at the narrow end of the passage I know you will look back and sigh a last regret for the flesh that flashed past your spirit in flight. You always had a restless eye. Your choice has my blessing. (*To the* **Women**.) Take the good news to our daughter and make her ready. (*Some* **Women** *go off.*)

Elesin Your eyes were clouded at first.

Iyaloja   Not for long. It is those who stand at the gateway of the great change to whose cry we must pay heed. And then, think of this – it makes the mind tremble. The fruit of such a union is rare. It will be neither of this world nor of the next. Nor of the one behind us. As if the timelessness of the ancestor world and the unborn have joined spirits to wring an issue of the elusive being of passage . . . Elesin!

Elesin   I am here. What is it?

Iyaloja   Did you hear all I said just now?

Elesin   Yes.

Iyaloja   The living must eat and drink. When the moment comes, don't turn the food to rodents' droppings in their mouth. Don't let them taste the ashes of the world when they step out at dawn to breathe the morning dew.

Elesin   This doubt is unworthy of you Iyaloja.

Iyaloja   Eating the awusa nut is not so difficult as drinking water afterwards.

Elesin
The waters of the bitter stream are honey to a man
Whose tongue has savoured all.

Iyaloja   No one knows when the ants desert their home; they leave the mound intact. The swallow is never seen to peck holes in its nest when it is time to move with the season. There are always throngs of humanity behind the leave-taker. The rain should not come through the roof for them, the wind must not blow through the walls at night.

Elesin   I refuse to take offence.

Iyaloja   You wish to travel light. Well, the earth is yours. But be sure the seed you leave in it attracts no curse.

Elesin   You really mistake my person Iyaloja.

Iyaloja   I said nothing. Now we must go prepare your bridal chamber. Then these same hands will lay your shrouds.

Elesin (*exasperated*) Must you be so blunt? (*Recovers.*) Well, weave your shrouds, but let the fingers of my bride seal my eyelids with earth and wash my body.

Iyaloja Prepare yourself Elesin.

She gets up to leave. At that moment the **Women** *return, leading the* **Bride**. **Elesin**'s *face glows with pleasure. He flicks the sleeves of his agbada with renewed confidence and steps forward to meet the group. As the girl kneels before* **Iyaloja**, *lights fade out on the scene.*

Scene Two

The verandah of the District Officer's bungalow. A tango is playing from an old hand-cranked gramophone and, glimpsed through the wide windows and doors which open onto the forestage verandah, are the shapes of **Simon Pilkings** *and his wife,* **Jane**, *tangoing in and out of shadows in the living-room. They are wearing what is immediately apparent as some form of fancy-dress. The dance goes on for some moments and then the figure of a 'Native Administration' policeman emerges and climbs up the steps onto the verandah. He peeps through and observes the dancing couple, reacting with what is obviously a long-standing bewilderment. He stiffens suddenly, his expression changes to one of disbelief and horror. In his excitement he upsets a flower-pot and attracts the attention of the couple. They stop dancing.*

Pilkings Is there anyone out there?

Jane I'll turn off the gramophone.

Pilkings (*approaching the verandah*) I'm sure I heard something fall over. (*The constable retreats slowly, open-mouthed as* **Pilkings** *approaches the verandah.*) Oh it's you Amusa. Why didn't you just knock instead of knocking things over?

Amusa (*stammers badly and points a shaky finger at his dress*) Mista Pirinkin . . . Mista Pirinkin . . .

Pilkings What is the matter with you?

Jane (*emerging*) Who is it dear? Oh, Amusa . . .

Pilkings   Yes it's Amusa, and acting most strangely.

Amusa (*his attention now transferred to* **Jane Pilkings**)
Mammadam . . . you too!

Pilkings   What the hell is the matter with you man!

Jane   Your costume darling. Our fancy-dress.

Pilkings   Oh hell, I'd forgotten all about that. (*Lifts the face
mask over his head showing his face. His wife follows suit.*)

Jane   I think you've shocked his big pagan heart bless him.

Pilkings   Nonsense, he's a Moslem. Come on Amusa, you
don't believe in all that nonsense do you? I thought you were
a good Moslem.

Amusa   Mista Pirinkin, I beg you sir, what you think you do
with that dress? It belong to dead cult, not for human being.

Pilkings   Oh Amusa, what a let-down you are. I swear by
you at the club you know – thank God for Amusa, he doesn't
believe in any mumbo-jumbo. And now look at you!

Amusa   Mista Pirinkin, I beg you, take it off. Is not good
for man like you to touch that cloth.

Pilkings   Well, I've got it on. And what's more Jane and I
have bet on it we're taking first prize at the ball. Now, if you
can just pull yourself together and tell me what you wanted to
see me about . . .

Amusa   Sir, I cannot talk this matter to you in that dress. I
no fit.

Pilkings   What's that rubbish again?

Jane   He is dead earnest too Simon. I think you'll have to
handle this delicately.

Pilkings   Delicately my. . . ! Look here Amusa, I think this
little joke has gone far enough hm? Let's have some sense.
You seem to forget that you are a police officer in the service
of His Majesty's Government. I order you to report your

business at once or face disciplinary action.

Amusa Sir, it is a matter of death. How can man talk
against death to person in uniform of death? Is like talking
against government to person in uniform of police. Please sir,
I go and come back.

Pilkings (*roars*) Now!

Amusa *switches his gaze to the ceiling suddenly, remains mute.*

Jane Oh Amusa, what is there to be scared of in the
costume? You saw it confiscated last month from those *egungun*
men who were creating trouble in town. You helped arrest the
cult leaders yourself – if the juju didn't harm you at the time
how could it possibly harm you now? And merely by looking
at it?

Amusa (*without looking down*) Madam, I arrest the ringleaders
who make trouble but me I no touch *egungun*. That *egungun*
inself, I no touch. And I no abuse 'am. I arrest ringleader but
I treat *egungun* with respect.

Pilkings It's hopeless. We'll merely end up missing the best
part of the ball. When they get this way there is nothing you
can do. It's simply hammering against a brick wall. Write
your report or whatever it is on that pad Amusa and take
yourself out of here. Come on Jane. We only upset his
delicate sensibilities by remaining here.

Amusa *waits for them to leave, then writes in the notebook, somewhat
laboriously. Drumming from the direction of the town wells up.* **Amusa**
listens, makes a movement as if he wants to recall **Pilkings** *but
changes his mind. Completes his note and goes. A few moments later*
Pilkings *emerges, picks up the pad and reads.*

Pilkings Jane!

Jane (*from the bedroom*) Coming darling. Nearly ready.

Pilkings Never mind being ready, just listen to this.

Jane What is it?

Pilkings Amusa's report. Listen. 'I have to report that it come to my information that one prominent chief, namely, the Elesin Oba, is to commit death tonight as a result of native custom. Because this is criminal offence I await further instruction at charge office. Sergeant Amusa.'

Jane *comes out onto the verandah while he is reading.*

Jane Did I hear you say commit death?

Pilkings Obviously he means murder.

Jane You mean a ritual murder?

Pilkings Must be. You think you've stamped it all out but it's always lurking under the surface somewhere.

Jane Oh. Does it mean we are not getting to the ball at all?

Pilkings No-o. I'll have the man arrested. Everyone remotely involved. In any case there may be nothing to it. Just rumours.

Jane Really? I thought you found Amusa's rumours generally reliable.

Pilkings That's true enough. But who knows what may have been giving him the scare lately. Look at his conduct tonight.

Jane (*laughing*) You have to admit he had his own peculiar logic. (*Deepens her voice.*) How can man talk against death to person in uniform of death? (*Laughs.*) Anyway, you can't go into the police station dressed like that.

Pilkings I'll send Joseph with instructions. Damn it, what a confounded nuisance!

Jane But don't you think you should talk first to the man, Simon?

Pilkings Do you want to go to the ball or not?

Jane Darling, why are you getting rattled? I was only trying to be intelligent. It seems hardly fair just to lock up a man –

and a chief at that – simply on the er ... what is the legal word again? – uncorroborated word of a sergeant.

Pilkings Well, that's easily decided. Joseph!

Joseph (*from within*) Yes master.

Pilkings You're quite right of course, I am getting rattled. Probably the effect of those bloody drums. Do you hear how they go on and on?

Jane I wondered when you'd notice. Do you suppose it has something to do with this affair?

Pilkings Who knows? They always find an excuse for making a noise ... (*Thoughtfully.*) Even so ...

Jane Yes Simon?

Pilkings It's different Jane. I don't think I've heard this particular – sound – before. Something unsettling about it.

Jane I thought all bush drumming sounded the same.

Pilkings Don't tease me now Jane. This may be serious.

Jane I'm sorry. (*Gets up and throws her arms around his neck. Kisses him. The houseboy enters, retreats and knocks.*)

Pilkings (*wearily*) Oh, come in Joseph! I don't know where you pick up all these elephantine notions of tact. Come over here.

Joseph Sir?

Pilkings Joseph, are you a Christian or not?

Joseph Yessir.

Pilkings Does seeing me in this outfit bother you?

Joseph No sir, it has no power.

Pilkings Thank God for some sanity at last. Now Joseph, answer me on the honour of a Christian – what is supposed to be going on in town tonight?

Joseph Tonight sir? You mean the chief who is going to kill himself?

Pilkings What?

Jane What do you mean, kill himself?

Pilkings You do mean he is going to kill somebody don't you?

Joseph No master. He will not kill anybody and no one will kill him. He will simply die.

Jane But why Joseph?

Joseph It is native law and custom. The King die last month. Tonight is his burial. But before they can bury him, the Elesin must die so as to accompany him to heaven.

Pilkings I seem to be fated to clash more often with that man than with any of the other chiefs.

Joseph He is the King's Chief Horseman.

Pilkings (*in a resigned way*) I know.

Jane Simon, what's the matter?

Pilkings It would have to be him!

Jane Who is he?

Pilkings Don't you remember? He's that chief with whom I had a scrap some three or four years ago. I helped his son get to a medical school in England, remember? He fought tooth and nail to prevent it.

Jane Oh now I remember. He was that very sensitive young man. What was his name again?

Pilkings Olunde. Haven't replied to his last letter come to think of it. The old pagan wanted him to stay and carry on some family tradition or the other. Honestly I couldn't understand the fuss he made. I literally had to help the boy escape from close confinement and load him onto the next boat. A most intelligent boy, really bright.

Jane   I rather thought he was much too sensitive you know. The kind of person you feel should be a poet munching rose petals in Bloomsbury.

Pilkings   Well, he's going to make a first-class doctor. His mind is set on that. And as long as he wants my help he is welcome to it.

Jane (*after a pause*)   Simon.

Pilkings   Yes?

Jane   This boy, he was the eldest son wasn't he?

Pilkings   I'm not sure. Who could tell with that old ram?

Jane   Do you know, Joseph?

Joseph   Oh yes madam. He was the eldest son. That's why Elesin cursed master good and proper. The eldest son is not supposed to travel away from the land.

Jane (*giggling*)   Is that true Simon? Did he really curse you good and proper?

Pilkings   By all accounts I should be dead by now.

Joseph   Oh no, master is white man. And good Christian. Black man juju can't touch master.

Jane   If he was his eldest, it means that he would be the Elesin to the next king. It's a family thing isn't it Joseph?

Joseph   Yes madam. And if this Elesin had died before the King, his eldest son must take his place.

Jane   That would explain why the old chief was so mad you took the boy away.

Pilkings   Well it makes me all the more happy I did.

Jane   I wonder if he knew.

Pilkings   Who? Oh, you mean Olunde?

Jane   Yes. Was that why he was so determined to get away? I wouldn't stay if I knew I was trapped in such a horrible custom.

Pilkings (*thoughtfully*) No, I don't think he knew. At least he gave no indication. But you couldn't really tell with him. He was rather close you know, quite unlike most of them. Didn't give much away, not even to me.

Jane Aren't they all rather close, Simon?

Pilkings These natives here? Good gracious. They'll open their mouths and yap with you about their family secrets before you can stop them. Only the other day . . .

Jane But Simon, do they really give anything away? I mean, anything that really counts. This affair for instance, we didn't know they still practised that custom did we?

Pilkings Ye-e-es, I suppose you're right there. Sly, devious bastards.

Joseph (*stiffly*) Can I go now master? I have to clean the kitchen.

Pilkings What? Oh, you can go. Forgot you were still there.

Joseph *goes.*

Jane Simon, you really must watch your language. Bastard isn't just a simple swear-word in these parts, you know.

Pilkings Look, just when did you become a social anthropologist, that's what I'd like to know.

Jane I'm not claiming to know anything. I just happen to have overheard quarrels among the servants. That's how I know they consider it a smear.

Pilkings I thought the extended family system took care of all that. Elastic family, no bastards.

Jane (*shrugs*) Have it your own way.

Awkward silence. The drumming increases in volume. **Jane** *gets up suddenly, restless.*

That drumming Simon, do you think it might really be
connected with this ritual? It's been going on all evening.

Pilkings   Let's ask our native guide. Joseph! Just a minute
Joseph. (**Joseph** *re-enters*.) What's the drumming about?

Joseph   I don't know master.

Pilkings   What do you mean you don't know? It's only two
years since your conversion. Don't tell me all that holy water
nonsense also wiped out your tribal memory.

Joseph (*visibly shocked*)   Master!

Jane   Now you've done it.

Pilkings   What have I done now?

Jane   Never mind. Listen Joseph, just tell me this. Is that
drumming connected with dying or anything of that nature?

Joseph   Madam, this is what I am trying to say: I am not
sure. It sounds like the death of a great chief and then, it
sounds like the wedding of a great chief. It really mix me up.

Pilkings   Oh get back to the kitchen. A fat lot of help you
are.

Joseph   Yes master. (*Goes.*)

Jane   Simon . . .

Pilkings   All right, all right. I'm in no mood for preaching.

Jane   It isn't my preaching you have to worry about, it's the
preaching of the missionaries who preceded you here. When
they make converts they really convert them. Calling holy
water nonsense to our Joseph is really like insulting the Virgin
Mary before a Roman Catholic. He's going to hand in his
notice tomorrow you mark my word.

Pilkings   Now you're being ridiculous.

Jane   Am I? What are you willing to bet that tomorrow we
are going to be without a steward-boy? Did you see his face?

Pilkings I am more concerned about whether or not we will be one native chief short by tomorrow. Christ! Just listen to those drums. (*He strides up and down, undecided.*)

Jane (*getting up*) I'll change and make up some supper.

Pilkings What's that?

Jane Simon, it's obvious we have to miss this ball.

Pilkings Nonsense. It's the first bit of real fun the European club has managed to organise for over a year, I'm damned if I'm going to miss it. And it is a rather special occasion. Doesn't happen every day.

Jane You know this business has to be stopped Simon. And you are the only man who can do it.

Pilkings I don't have to stop anything. If they want to throw themselves off the top of a cliff or poison themselves for the sake of some barbaric custom what is that to me? If it were ritual murder or something like that I'd be duty-bound to do something. I can't keep an eye on all the potential suicides in this province. And as for that man – believe me it's good riddance.

Jane (*laughs*) I know you better than that Simon. You are going to have to do something to stop it – after you've finished blustering.

Pilkings (*shouts after her*) And suppose after all it's only a wedding? I'd look a proper fool if I interrupted a chief on his honeymoon, wouldn't I? (*Resumes his angry stride, slows down.*) Ah well, who can tell what those chiefs actually do on their honeymoon anyway? (*He takes up the pad and scribbles rapidly on it.*) Joseph! Joseph! Joseph! (*Some moments later* **Joseph** *puts in a sulky appearance.*) Did you hear me call you? Why the hell didn't you answer?

Joseph I didn't hear master.

Pilkings You didn't hear me! How come you are here then?

Joseph (*stubbornly*)   I didn't hear master.

Pilkings (*controls himself with an effort*)   We'll talk about it in the morning. I want you to take this note directly to Sergeant Amusa. You'll find him at the charge office. Get on your bicycle and race there with it. I expect you back in twenty minutes exactly. Twenty minutes, is that clear?

Joseph   Yes master (*Going.*)

Pilkings   Oh er . . . Joseph.

Joseph   Yes master?

Pilkings (*between gritted teeth*)   Er . . . forget what I said just now. The holy water is not nonsense. *I* was talking nonsense.

Joseph   Yes master. (*Goes.*)

Jane (*pokes her head round the door*)   Have you found him?

Pilkings   Found who?

Jane   Joseph. Weren't you shouting for him?

Pilkings   Oh yes, he turned up finally.

Jane   You sounded desperate. What was it all about?

Pilkings   Oh nothing. I just wanted to apologise to him. Assure him that the holy water isn't really nonsense.

Jane   Oh? And how did he take it?

Pilkings   Who the hell gives a damn! I had a sudden vision of our Very Reverend Macfarlane drafting another letter of complaint to the Resident about my unchristian language towards his parishioners.

Jane   Oh I think he's given up on you by now.

Pilkings   Don't be too sure. And anyway, I wanted to make sure Joseph didn't 'lose' my note on the way. He looked sufficiently full of the holy crusade to do some such thing.

Jane   If you've finished exaggerating, come and have something to eat.

Pilkings No, put it all away. We can still get to the ball.

Jane Simon . . .

Pilkings Get your costume back on. Nothing to worry about. I've instructed Amusa to arrest the man and lock him up.

Jane But that station is hardly secure Simon. He'll soon get his friends to help him escape.

Pilkings A-ah, that's where I have out-thought you. I'm not having him put in the station cell. Amusa will bring him right here and lock him up in my study. And he'll stay with him till we get back. No one will dare come here to incite him to anything.

Jane How clever of you darling. I'll get ready.

Pilkings Hey.

Jane Yes darling.

Pilkings I have a surprise for you. I was going to keep it until we actually got to the ball.

Jane What is it?

Pilkings You know the Prince is on a tour of the colonies don't you? Well, he docked in the capital only this morning but he is already at the Residency. He is going to grace the ball with his presence later tonight.

Jane Simon! Not really.

Pilkings Yes he is. He's been invited to give away the prizes and he has agreed. You must admit old Engleton is the best Club Secretary we ever had. Quick off the mark that lad.

Jane But how thrilling.

Pilkings The other provincials are going to be damned envious.

Jane I wonder what he'll come as.

Pilkings   Oh I don't know. As a coat-of-arms perhaps. Anyway it won't be anything to touch this.

Jane   Well that's lucky. If we are to be presented I won't have to start looking for a pair of gloves. It's all sewn on.

Pilkings (*laughing*)   Quite right. Trust a woman to think of that. Come on, let's get going.

Jane (*rushing off*)   Won't be a second. (*Stops.*) Now I see why you've been so edgy all evening. I thought you weren't handling this affair with your usual brilliance – to begin with that is.

Pilkings (*his mood is much improved*)   Shut up woman and get your things on.

Jane   All right boss, coming.

Pilkings *suddenly begins to hum the tango to which they were dancing before. Starts to execute a few practice steps. Lights fade.*

Scene Three

A swelling, agitated hum of women's voices rises immediately in the background. The lights come on and we see the frontage of a converted cloth stall in the market. The floor leading up to the entrance is covered in rich velvets and woven cloth. The **Women** *come on stage, borne backwards by the determined progress of Sergeant* **Amusa** *and his two constables who already have their batons out and use them as a pressure against the* **Women***. At the edge of the cloth-covered floor, however, the* **Women** *take a determined stand and block all further progress of the men. They begin to tease them mercilessly.*

Amusa   I am tell you women for last time to commot my road. I am here on official business.

Woman   Official business you white man's eunuch? Official business is taking place where you want to go and it's a business you wouldn't understand.

Woman (*makes a quick tug at the constable's baton*)   That doesn't

fool anyone you know. It's the one you carry under your
government knickers that counts. (*She bends low as if to peep
under the baggy shorts. The embarrassed constable quickly puts his knees
together. The* **Women** *roar.*)

Woman   You mean there is nothing there at all?

Woman   Oh there was something. You know that handbell
which the white man uses to summon his servants . . . ?

Amusa (*he manages to preserve some dignity throughout*)   I hope you
women know that interfering with officer in execution of his
duty is criminal offence.

Woman   Interfere? He says we're interfering with him. You
foolish man we're telling you there's nothing to interfere with.

Amusa   I am order you now to clear the road.

Woman   What road? The one your father built?

Woman   You are a policeman not so? Then you know what
they call trespassing in court. Or – (*Pointing to the cloth-lined
steps.*) – do you think that kind of road is built for every kind
of feet.

Woman   Go back and tell the white man who sent you to
come himself.

Amusa   If I go I will come back with reinforcement. And we
will all return carrying weapons.

Woman   Oh, now I understand. Before they can put on
those knickers the white man first cuts off their weapons.

Woman   What a cheek! You mean you come here to show
power to women and you don't even have a weapon.

Amusa (*shouting above the laughter*)   For the last time I warn
you women to clear the road.

Woman   To where?

Amusa   To that hut. I know he dey dere.

Woman   Who?

Amusa The chief who call himself Elesin Oba.

Woman You ignorant man. It is not he who calls himself Elesin Oba, it is his blood that says it. As it called out to his father before him and will to his son after him. And that is in spite of everything your white man can do.

Woman Is it not the same ocean that washes this land and the white man's land? Tell your white man he can hide our son away as long as he likes. When the time comes for him, the same ocean will bring him back.

Amusa The government say dat kin' ting must stop.

Woman Who will stop it? You? Tonight our husband and father will prove himself greater than the laws of strangers.

Amusa I tell you nobody go prove anyting tonight or anytime. Is ignorant and criminal to prove dat kin' prove.

Iyaloja (*entering from the hut. She is accompanied by a group of young* **Girls** *who have been attending the* **Bride**) What is it Amusa? Why do you come here to disturb the happiness of others.

Amusa Madame Iyaloja, I glad you come. You know me, I no like trouble but duty is duty. I am here to arrest Elesin for criminal intent. Tell these women to stop obstructing me in the performance of my duty.

Iyaloja And you? What gives you the right to obstruct our leader of men in the performance of his duty.

Amusa What kin' duty be dat one Iyaloja.

Iyaloja What kin' duty? What kin' duty does a man have to his new bride?

Amusa (*bewildered, looks at the* **Women** *and at the entrance to the hut*) Iyaloja, is it wedding you call dis kin' ting?

Iyaloja You have wives haven't you? Whatever the white man has done to you he hasn't stopped you having wives. And if he has, at least he is married. If you don't know what a marriage is, go and ask him to tell you.

Amusa   This no to wedding.

Iyaloja   And ask him at the same time what he would have done if anyone had come to disturb him on his wedding night.

Amusa   Iyaloja, I say dis no to wedding.

Iyaloja   You want to look inside the bridal chamber? You want to see for yourself how a man cuts the virgin knot?

Amusa   Madam . . .

Woman   Perhaps his wives are still waiting for him to learn.

Amusa   Iyaloja, make you tell dese women make den no insult me again. If I hear dat kin' insult once more . . .

Girl (*pushing her way through*)   You will do what?

Girl   He's out of his mind. It's our mothers you're talking to, do you know that? Not to any illiterate villager you can bully and terrorise. How dare you intrude here anyway?

Girl   What a cheek, what impertinence!

Girl   You've treated them too gently. Now let them see what it is to tamper with the mothers of this market.

Girl   Your betters dare not enter the market when the women say no!

Girl   Haven't you learnt that yet, you jester in khaki and starch?

Iyaloja   Daughters . . .

Girl   No no Iyaloja, leave us to deal with him. He no longer knows his mother, we'll teach him.

With a sudden movement they snatch the batons of the two constables. They begin to hem them in.

Girl   What next? We have your batons? What next? What are you going to do?

With equally swift movements they knock off their hats.

Girl Move if you dare. We have your hats, what will you do about it? Didn't the white man teach you to take off your hats before women?

Iyaloja It's a wedding night. It's a night of joy for us. Peace . . .

Girl Not for him. Who asked him here?

Girl Does he dare go to the Residency without an invitation?

Girl Not even where the servants eat the left-overs.

Girls (*in turn. In an 'English' accent*) Well well it's Mister Amusa. Were you invited? (*Play-acting to one another. The older* **Women** *encourage them with their titters.*)
—Your invitation card please?
—Who are you? Have we been introduced?
—And who did you say you were?
—Sorry, I didn't quite catch your name.
—May I take your hat?
—If you insist. May I take yours? (*Exchanging the policemen's hats.*)
—How very kind of you.
—Not at all. Won't you sit down?
—After you.
—Oh no.
—I insist.
—You're most gracious.
—And how do you find the place?
—The natives are all right.
—Friendly?
—Tractable.
—Not a teeny-weeny bit restless?
—Well, a teeny-weeny bit restless.
—One might even say, difficult?
—Indeed one might be tempted to say, difficult.
—But you do manage to cope?
—Yes indeed I do. I have a rather faithful ox called Amusa.
—He's loyal?

—Absolutely.
—Lay down his life for you what?
—Without a moment's thought.
—Had one like that once. Trust him with my life.
—Mostly of course they are liars.
—Never known a native to tell the truth.
—Does it get rather close around here?
—It's mild for this time of the year.
—But the rains may still come.
—They are late this year aren't they?
—They are keeping African time.
—Ha ha ha ha.
—Ha ha ha ha.
—The humidity is what gets me.
—It used to be whisky.
—Ha ha ha ha.
—Ha ha ha ha.
—What's your handicap old chap?
—Is there racing by golly?
—Splendid golf course, you'll like it.
—I'm beginning to like it already.
—And a European club, exclusive.
—You've kept the flag flying.
—We do our best for the old country.
—It's a pleasure to serve.
—Another whisky old chap?
—You are indeed too too kind.
—Not at all sir. Where is that boy? (*With a sudden bellow.*)
Sergeant!

Amusa (*snaps to attention*)   Yessir!

The **Women** *collapse with laughter.*

Girl   Take your men out of here.

Amusa (*realising the trick, he rages from loss of face*)   I'm give you
warning . . .

Girl   All right then. Off with his knickers! (*They surge slowly
forward.*)

Iyaloja Daughters, please.

Amusa (*squaring himself for defence*) The first woman wey touch me.

Iyaloja My children, I beg of you . . .

Girl Then tell him to leave this market. This is the home of our mothers. We don't want the eater of white left-overs at the feast their hands have prepared.

Iyaloja You heard them Amusa. You had better go.

Girl Now!

Amusa (*commencing his retreat*) We dey go now, but make you no say we no warn you.

Girl Now!

Girl Before we read the riot act – you should know all about that.

Amusa Make we go. (*They depart, more precipitately.*)

The **Women** *strike their palms across in the gesture of wonder.*

Women Do they teach you all that at school?

Woman And to think I nearly kept Apinke away from the place.

Woman Did you hear them? Did you see how they mimicked the white man?

Woman The voices exactly. Hey, there are wonders in this world!

Iyaloja Well, our elders have said it: Dada may be weak, but he has a younger sibling who is truly fearless.

Woman The next time the white man shows his face in this market I will set Wuraola on his tail.

A **Woman** *bursts into song and dance of euphoria – 'Tani l'awa o*

l'ogbeja? Kayi! A l'ogbeja. Omo Kekere l'ogbeja.[1] *The rest of the*
Women *join in, some placing the* **Girls** *on their back like infants,*
others dancing round them. The dance becomes general, mounting in
excitement. **Elesin** *appears, in wrapper only. In his hands a white velvet*
cloth folded loosely as if it held some delicate object. He cries out.

Elesin   Oh you mothers of beautiful brides! (*The dancing stops.*
They turn and see him, and the object in his hands. **Iyaloja** *approaches*
and gently takes the cloth from him.) Take it. It is no mere virgin
stain, but the union of life and the seeds of passage. My vital
flow, the last from this flesh is intermingled with the promise
of future life. All is prepared. Listen! (*A steady drumbeat from the*
distance.) Yes. It is nearly time. The King's dog has been killed.
The King's favourite horse is about to follow his master. My
brother chiefs know their task and perform it well. (*He listens*
again.)

The **Bride** *emerges, stands shyly by the door. He turns to her.*

Elesin   Our marriage is not yet wholly fulfilled. When earth
and passage wed, the consummation is complete only when
there are grains of earth on the eyelids of passage. Stay by me
till then. My faithful drummers, do me your last service. This
is where I have chosen to do my leave-taking, in this heart of
life, this hive which contains the swarm of the world in its
small compass. This is where I have known love and laughter
away from the palace. Even the richest food cloys when eaten
days on end; in the market, nothing ever cloys. Listen. (*They*
listen to the drums.) They have begun to seek out the heart of
the King's favourite horse. Soon it will ride in its bolt of raffia
with the dog at its feet. Together they will ride on the
shoulders of the King's grooms through the pulse centres of
the town. They know it is here I shall await them. I have told
them (*His eyes appear to cloud. He passes his hand over them as if to*
clear his sight. He gives a faint smile.) It promises well; just then I
felt my spirit's eagerness. The kite makes for wide spaces and
the wind creeps up behind its tail; can the kite say less than –
thank you, the quicker the better? But wait a while my spirit.

[1] 'Who says we haven't a defender? Silence! We have our defenders. Little children are
our champions.'

Wait. Wait for the coming of the courier of the King. Do you know, friends, the horse is born to this one destiny, to bear the burden that is man upon its back. Except for this night, this night alone when the spotless stallion will ride in triumph on the back of man. In the time of my father I witnessed the strange sight. Perhaps tonight also I shall see it for the last time. If they arrive before the drums beat for me, I shall tell them to let the Alafin know I follow swiftly. If they come after the drums have sounded, why then, all is well for I have gone ahead. Our spirits shall fall in step along the great passage. (*He listens to the drums. He seems again to be falling into a state of semi-hypnosis; his eyes scan the sky but it is in a kind of daze. His voice is a little breathless.*) The moon has fed, a glow from its full stomach fills the sky and air, but I cannot tell where is that gateway through which I must pass. My faithful friends, let our feet touch together this last time, lead me into the other market with sounds that cover my skin with down yet make my limbs strike earth like a thoroughbred. Dear mothers, let me dance into the passage even as I have lived beneath your roofs.

He comes down progressively among them. They make way for him, the drummers playing. His dance is one of solemn, regal motions, each gesture of the body is made with a solemn finality. The **Women** *join him, their steps a somewhat more fluid version of his. Beneath the* **Praise-Singer**'s *exhortations the* **Women** *dirge 'Ale le le, awo mi lo'.*

Praise-Singer
Elesin Alafin, can you hear my voice?

Elesin
Faintly, my friend, faintly.

Praise-Singer
Elesin Alafin, can you hear my call?

Elesin
Faintly my King, faintly.

Praise-Singer
Is your memory sound Elesin?

Shall my voice be a blade of grass and
Tickle the armpit of the past?

Elesin

My memory needs no prodding but
What do you wish to say to me?

Praise-Singer

Only what has been spoken. Only what concerns
The dying wish of the father of all.

Elesin

It is buried like seed-yam in my mind.
This is the season of quick rains, the harvest
Is this moment due for gathering.

Praise-Singer

If you cannot come, I said, swear
You'll tell my favourite horse. I shall
Ride on through the gates alone.

Elesin

Elesin's message will be read
Only when his loyal heart no longer beats.

Praise-Singer

If you cannot come Elesin, tell my dog.
I cannot stay the keeper too long
At the gate.

Elesin

A dog does not outrun the hand
That feeds it meat. A horse that throws its rider
Slows down to a stop. Elesin Alafin
Trusts no beasts with messages between
A king and his companion.

Praise-Singer

If you get lost my dog will track
The hidden path to me.

Elesin

The seven-way crossroads confuses

Only the stranger. The Horseman of the King
Was born in the recesses of the house.

Praise-Singer

I know the wickedness of men. If there is
Weight on the loose end of your sash, such weight
As no mere man can shift; if your sash is earthed
By evil minds who mean to part us at the last . . .

Elesin

My sash is of the deep purple *alari*;
It is no tethering-rope. The elephant
Trails no tethering-rope; that king
Is not yet crowned who will peg an elephant –
Not even you my friend and King.

Praise-Singer

And yet this fear will not depart from me,
The darkness of this new abode is deep –
Will your human eyes suffice?

Elesin

In a night which falls before our eyes
However deep, we do not miss our way.

Praise-Singer

Shall I now not acknowledge I have stood
Where wonders met their end? The elephant deserves
Better than that we say 'I have caught
A glimpse of something'. If we see the tamer
Of the forest let us say plainly, we have seen
An elephant.

Elesin (*his voice is drowsy*)

I have freed myself of earth and now
It's getting dark. Strange voices guide my feet.

Praise-Singer

The river is never so high that the eyes
Of a fish are covered. The night is not so dark
That the albino fails to find his way. A child
Returning homewards craves no leading by the hand.

Gracefully does the mask regain his grove at the end of the
    day . . .
Gracefully. Gracefully does the mask dance
Homeward at the end of the day, gracefully . . .

Elesin's trance appears to be deepening, his steps heavier.

Iyaloja
It is the death of war that kills the valiant,
Death of water is how the swimmer goes.
It is the death of markets that kills the trader
And death of indecision takes the idle away.
The trade of the cutlass blunts its edge
And the beautiful die the death of beauty.
It takes an Elesin to die the death of death . . .
Only Elesin . . . dies the unknowable death of death . . .
Gracefully, gracefully does the horseman regain
The stables at the end of day, gracefully . . .

Praise-Singer   How shall I tell what my eyes have seen?
The Horseman gallops on before the courier, how shall I tell
what my eyes have seen? He says a dog may be confused by
new scents of beings he never dreamt of, so he must precede
the dog to heaven. He says a horse may stumble on strange
boulders and be lamed, so he races on before the horse to
heaven. It is best, he says, to trust no messenger who may
falter at the outer gate; oh how shall I tell what my ears have
heard? But do you hear me still Elesin, do you hear your
faithful one?

*Elesin in his motions appears to feel for a direction of sound, subtly,
but he only sinks deeper into his trance-dance.*

Praise-Singer   Elesin Alafin, I no longer sense your flesh.
The drums are changing now but you have gone far ahead of
the world. It is not yet noon in heaven; let those who claim it
is begin their own journey home. So why must you rush like
an impatient bride: why do you race to desert your Olohun-
iyo?

Elesin is now sunk fully deep in his trance, there is no longer sign of any awareness of his surroundings.

Praise-Singer   Does the deep voice of *gbedu* cover you then,
like the passage of royal elephants? Those drums that brook
no rivals, have they blocked the passage to your ears that my
voice passes into wind, a mere leaf floating in the night? Is
your flesh lightened Elesin, is that lump of earth I slid
between your slippers to keep you longer slowly sifting from
your feet? Are the drums on the other side now tuning skin to
skin with ours in *osugbo*? Are there sounds there I cannot hear,
do footsteps surround you which pound the earth like *gbedu*,
roll like thunder round the dome of the world? Is the darkness
gathering in your head Elesin? Is there now a streak of light
at the end of the passage, a light I dare not look upon? Does
it reveal whose voices we often heard, whose touches we often
felt, whose wisdoms come suddenly into the mind when the
wisest have shaken their heads and murmured, It cannot be
done? Elesin Alafin, don't think I do not know why your lips
are heavy, why your limbs are drowsy as palm oil in the cold
of harmattan. I would call you back but when the elephant
heads for the jungle, the tail is too small a handhold for the
hunter that would pull him back. The sun that heads for the
sea no longer heeds the prayers of the farmer. When the river
begins to taste the salt of the ocean, we no longer know what
deity to call on, the river-god or Olokun. No arrow flies back
to the string, the child does not return through the same
passage that gave it birth. Elesin Oba, can you hear me at
all? Your eyelids are glazed like a courtesan's, is it that you
see the dark groom and master of life? And will you see my
father? Will you tell him that I stayed with you to the last?
Will my voice ring in your ears awhile, will you remember
Olohun-iyo even if the music on the other side surpasses his
mortal craft? But will they know you over there? Have they
eyes to gauge your worth, have they the heart to love you,
will they know what thoroughbred prances towards them in
caparisons of honour? If they do not Elesin, if any there cuts
your yam with a small knife, or pours you wine in a small
calabash, turn back and return to welcoming hands. If the
world were not greater than the wishes of Olohun-iyo, I

would not let you go . . .

He appears to break down. **Elesin** *dances on, completely in a trance. The dirge wells up louder and stronger.* **Elesin***'s dance does not lose its elasticity but his gestures become, if possible, even more weighty. Lights fade slowly on the scene.*

Scene Four

A masque. The front side of the stage is part of a wide corridor around the great hall of the Residency extending beyond vision into the rear and wings. It is redolent of the tawdry decadence of a far-flung but key imperial frontier. The couples in a variety of fancy-dress are ranged around the walls, gazing in the same direction. The guest-of-honour is about to make an appearance. A portion of the local police brass band with its white conductor is just visible. At last, the entrance of Royalty. The band plays 'Rule Britannia', badly, beginning long before he is visible. The couples bow and curtsey as he passes by them. Both he and his companions are dressed in seventeenth-century European costume. Following behind are the **Resident** *and his partner similarly attired. As they gain the end of the hall where the orchestra dais begins the music comes to an end. The* **Prince** *bows to the guests. The band strikes up a Viennese waltz and the* **Prince** *formally opens the floor. Several bars later the* **Resident** *and his companion follow suit. Others follow in appropriate pecking order. The orchestra's waltz rendition is not of the highest musical standard.*

Some time later the **Prince** *dances again into view and is settled into a corner by the* **Resident** *who then proceeds to select couples as they dance past for introduction, sometimes threading his way through the dancers to tap the lucky couple on the shoulder. Desperate efforts from many to ensure that they are recognised in spite of, perhaps, their costume. The ritual of introductions soon takes in* **Pilkings** *and his wife. The* **Prince** *is quite fascinated by their costume and they demonstrate the adaptations they have made to it, pulling down the mask to demonstrate how the egungun normally appears, then showing the various press-button controls they have innovated for the face flaps, the sleeves, etc. They demonstrate the dance steps and* *the guttural sounds made by the* egungun, *harass other dancers in the hall,* **Mrs Pilkings** *playing the 'restrainer' to* **Pilkings**' *manic darts. Everyone is highly entertained, the Royal Party especially who lead the applause.*

At this point a liveried footman comes in with a note on a salver and is intercepted almost absent-mindedly by the **Resident** *who takes the note and reads it. After polite coughs he succeeds in excusing the* **Pilkings** *from the* **Prince** *and takes them aside. The* **Prince** *considerately offers the* **Resident**'s *wife his hand and dancing is resumed.*

On their way out the **Resident** *gives an order to his* **Aide-de-Camp**. *They come into the side corridor where the* **Resident** *hands the note to* **Pilkings**.

Resident   As you see it says 'emergency' on the outside. I took the liberty of opening it because His Highness was obviously enjoying the entertainment. I didn't want to interrupt unless really necessary.

Pilkings   Yes, yes of course, sir.

Resident   Is it really as bad as it says? What's it all about?

Pilkings   Some strange custom they have, sir. It seems because the King is dead some important chief has to commit suicide.

Resident   The King? Isn't it the same one who died nearly a month ago?

Pilkings   Yes, sir.

Resident   Haven't they buried him yet?

Pilkings   They take their time about these things, sir. The pre-burial ceremonies last nearly thirty days. It seems tonight is the final night.

Resident   But what has it got to do with the market women? Why are they rioting? We've waived that troublesome tax haven't we?

Pilkings   We don't quite know that they are exactly rioting yet, sir. Sergeant Amusa is sometimes prone to exaggerations.

Resident He sounds desperate enough. That comes out even in his rather quaint grammar. Where is the man anyway? I asked my aide-de-camp to bring him here.

Pilkings They are probably looking in the wrong verandah. I'll fetch him myself.

Resident No no you stay here. Let your wife go and look for them. Do you mind my dear . . . ?

Jane Certainly not, your Excellency. (*Goes.*)

Resident You should have kept me informed, Pilkings. You realise how disastrous it would have been if things had erupted while His Highness was here.

Pilkings I wasn't aware of the whole business until tonight, sir.

Resident Nose to the ground Pilkings, nose to the ground. If we all let these little things slip past us where would the empire be eh? Tell me that. Where would we all be?

Pilkings (*low voice*) Sleeping peacefully at home I bet.

Resident What did you say, Pilkings?

Pilkings It won't happen again, sir.

Resident It mustn't, Pilkings. It mustn't. Where is that damned sergeant? I ought to get back to His Highness as quickly as possible and offer him some plausible explanation for my rather abrupt conduct. Can you think of one, Pilkings?

Pilkings You could tell him the truth, sir.

Resident I could? No no no Pilkings, that would never do. What! Go and tell him there is a riot just two miles away from him? This is supposed to be a secure colony of His Majesty, Pilkings.

Pilkings Yes, sir.

Resident Ah, there they are. No, these are not our native police. Are these the ring-leaders of the riot?

Pilkings Sir, these are my police officers.

Resident Oh, I beg your pardon officers. You do look a little ... I say, isn't there something missing in their uniform? I think they used to have some rather colourful sashes. If I remember rightly I recommended them myself in my young days in the service. A bit of colour always appeals to the natives, yes, I remember putting that in my report. Well well well, where are we? Make your report man.

Pilkings (*moves close to* **Amusa**, *between his teeth*) And let's have no more superstitious nonsense from you Amusa or I'll throw you in the guardroom for a month and feed you pork!

Resident What's that? What has pork to do with it?

Pilkings Sir, I was just warning him to be brief. I'm sure you are most anxious to hear his report.

Resident Yes yes yes of course. Come on man, speak up. Hey, didn't we give them some colourful fez hats with all those wavy things, yes, pink tassels ...

Pilkings Sir, I think if he was permitted to make his report we might find that he lost his hat in the riot.

Resident Ah yes indeed. I'd better tell His Highness that. Lost his hat in the riot, ha ha. He'll probably say well, as long as he didn't lose his head. (*Chuckles to himself.*) Don't forget to send me a report first thing in the morning young Pilkings.

Pilkings No, sir.

Resident And whatever you do, don't let things get out of hand. Keep a cool head and – nose to the ground Pilkings. (*Wanders off in the general direction of the hall.*)

Pilkings Yes, sir.

Aide-de-Camp Would you be needing me, sir?

Pilkings No thanks, Bob. I think His Excellency's need of you is greater than ours.

Aide-de-Camp   We have a detachment of soldiers from the capital, sir. They accompanied His Highness up here.

Pilkings   I doubt if it will come to that but, thanks, I'll bear it in mind. Oh, could you send an orderly with my cloak.

Aide-de-Camp   Very good, sir. (*Goes.*)

Pilkings   Now, sergeant.

Amusa   Sir . . . (*Makes an effort, stops dead. Eyes to the ceiling.*)

Pilkings   Oh, not again.

Amusa   I cannot against death to dead cult. This dress get power of dead.

Pilkings   All right, let's go. You are relieved of all further duty Amusa. Report to me first thing in the morning.

Jane   Shall I come, Simon?

Pilkings   No, there's no need for that. If I can get back later I will. Otherwise get Bob to bring you home.

Jane   Be careful Simon . . . I mean, be clever.

Pilkings   Sure I will. You two, come with me. (*As he turns to go, the clock in the Residency begins to chime.* **Pilkings** *looks at his watch then turns, horror-stricken, to stare at his wife. The same thought clearly occurs to her. He swallows hard. An orderly brings his cloak.*) It's midnight. I had no idea it was that late.

Jane   But surely . . . they don't count the hours the way we do. The moon, or something . . .

Pilkings   I am . . . not so sure.

He turns and breaks into a sudden run. The two constables follow, also at a run. **Amusa,** *who has kept his eyes on the ceiling throughout, waits until the last of the footsteps has faded out of hearing. He salutes suddenly, but without once looking in the direction of the woman.*

Amusa   Goodnight, madam.

Jane Oh. (*She hesitates.*) Amusa ... (*He goes off without seeming to have heard.*) Poor Simon ...

A figure emerges from the shadows, a young black man dressed in a sober western suit. He peeps into the hall, trying to make out the figures of the dancers.

Jane Who is that?

Olunde (*emerges into the light*) I didn't mean to startle you madam. I am looking for the District Officer.

Jane Wait a minute ... don't I know you? Yes, you are Olunde, the young man who ...

Olunde Mrs Pilkings! How fortunate. I came here to look for your husband.

Jane Olunde! Let's look at you. What a fine young man you've become. Grand but solemn. Good God, when did you return? Simon never said a word. But you do look well Olunde. Really!

Olunde You are ... well, you look quite well yourself Mrs Pilkings. From what little I can see of you.

Jane Oh, this. It's caused quite a stir I assure you, and not all of it very pleasant. You are not shocked I hope?

Olunde Why should I be? But don't you find it rather hot in there? Your skin must find it difficult to breathe.

Jane Well, it is a little hot I must confess, but it's all in a good cause.

Olunde What cause Mrs Pilkings?

Jane All this. The ball. And His Highness being here in person and all that.

Olunde (*mildly*) And that is the good cause for which you desecrate an ancestral mask?

Jane Oh, so you are shocked after all. How disappointing.

Olunde No I am not shocked, Mrs Pilkings. You forget that

I have now spent four years among your people. I discovered that you have no respect for what you do not understand.

Jane Oh. So you've returned with a chip on your shoulder. That's a pity Olunde. I am sorry.

An uncomfortable silence follows.

I take it then that you did not find you stay in England altogether edifying.

Olunde I don't say that. I found your people quite admirable in many ways, their conduct and courage in this war for instance.

Jane Ah yes, the war. Here of course it is all rather remote. From time to time we have a black-out drill just to remind us that there is a war on. And the rare convoy passes through on its way somewhere or on manoeuvres. Mind you there is the occasional bit of excitement like that ship that was blown up in the harbour.

Olunde Here? Do you mean through enemy action?

Jane Oh no, the war hasn't come that close. The captain did it himself. I don't quite understand it really. Simon tried to explain. The ship had to be blown up because it had become dangerous to other ships, even to the city itself. Hundreds of the coastal population would have died.

Olunde Maybe it was loaded with ammunition and had caught fire. Or some of those lethal gases they've been experimenting on.

Jane Something like that. The captain blew himself up with it. Deliberately. Simon said someone had to remain on board to light the fuse.

Olunde It must have been a very short fuse.

Jane (*shrugs*) I don't know much about it. Only that there was no other way to save lives. No time to devise anything else. The captain took the decision and carried it out.

Olunde   Yes . . . I quite believe it. I met men like that in England.

Jane   Oh just look at me! Fancy welcoming you back with such morbid news. Stale too. It was at least six months ago.

Olunde   I don't find it morbid at all. I find it rather inspiring. It is an affirmative commentary on life.

Jane   What is?

Olunde   That captain's self-sacrifice.

Jane   Nonsense. Life should never be thrown deliberately away.

Olunde   And the innocent people around the harbour?

Jane   Oh, how does one know? The whole thing was probably exaggerated anyway.

Olunde   That was a risk the captain couldn't take. But please Mrs Pilkings, do you think you could find your husband for me? I have to talk to him.

Jane   Simon? (*As she recollects for the first time the full significance of* **Olunde***'s presence.*) Simon is . . . there is a little problem in town. He was sent for. But . . . when did you arrive? Does Simon know you're here?

Olunde (*suddenly earnest*)   I need your help Mrs Pilkings. I've always found you somewhat more understanding than your husband. Please find him for me and when you do, you must help me talk to him.

Jane   I'm afraid I don't quite . . . follow you. Have you seen my husband already?

Olunde   I went to your house. Your houseboy told me you were here. (*He smiles.*) He even told me how I would recognise you and Mr Pilkings.

Jane   Then you must know what my husband is trying to do for you.

Olunde For me?

Jane For you. For your people. And to think he didn't even know you were coming back! But how do you happen to be here? Only this evening we were talking about you. We thought you were still four thousand miles away.

Olunde I was sent a cable.

Jane A cable? Who did? Simon? The business of your father didn't begin till tonight.

Olunde A relation sent it weeks ago, and it said nothing about my father. All it said was, Our King is dead. But I knew I had to return home at once so as to bury my father. I understood that.

Jane Well, thank God you don't have to go through that agony. Simon is going to stop it.

Olunde That's why I want to see him. He's wasting his time. And since he has been so helpful to me I don't want him to incur the enmity of our people. Especially over nothing.

Jane (*sits down open-mouthed*) You ... you Olunde!

Olunde Mrs Pilkings, I came home to bury my father. As soon as I heard the news I booked my passage home. In fact we were fortunate. We travelled in the same convoy as your Prince, so we had excellent protection.

Jane But you don't think your father is also entitled to whatever protection is available to him?

Olunde How can I make you understand? He *has* protection. No one can undertake what he does tonight without the deepest protection the mind can conceive. What can you offer him in place of his peace of mind, in place of the honour and veneration of his own people? What would you think of your Prince if he refused to accept the risk of losing his life on this voyage? This ... showing-the-flag tour of colonial possessions.

Jane I see. So it isn't just medicine you studied in England.

Olunde Yet another error into which your people fall. You believe that everything which appears to make sense was learnt from you.

Jane Not so fast Olunde. You have learnt to argue I can tell that, but I never said you made sense. However clearly you try to put it, it is still a barbaric custom. It is even worse – it's feudal! The King dies and a chieftain must be buried with him. How feudalistic can you get!

Olunde (*waves his hand towards the background. The* **Prince** *is dancing past again – to a different step – and all the guests are bowing and curtseying as he passes*) And this? Even in the midst of a devastating war, look at that. What name would you give to that?

Jane Therapy, British style. The preservation of sanity in the midst of chaos.

Olunde Others would call it decadence. However, it doesn't really interest me. You white races know how to survive; I've seen proof of that. By all logical and natural laws this war should end with all the white races wiping out one another, wiping out their so-called civilisation for all time and reverting to a state of primitivism the like of which has so far only existed in your imagination when you thought of us. I thought all that at the beginning. Then I slowly realised that your greatest art is the art of survival. But at least have the humility to let others survive in their own way.

Jane Through ritual suicide?

Olunde Is that worse than mass suicide? Mrs Pilkings, what do you call what those young men are sent to do by their generals in this war? Of course you have also mastered the art of calling things by names which don't remotely describe them.

Jane You talk! You people with your long-winded, roundabout way of making conversation.

Olunde   Mrs Pilkings, whatever we do, we never suggest that a thing is the opposite of what it really is. In your newsreels I heard defeats, thorough, murderous defeats described as strategic victories. No wait, it wasn't just on your newsreels. Don't forget I was attached to hospitals all the time. Hordes of your wounded passed through those wards. I spoke to them. I spent long evenings by their bedsides while they spoke terrible truths of the realities of that war. I know now how history is made.

Jane   But surely, in a war of this nature, for the morale of the nation you must expect . . .

Olunde   That a disaster beyond human reckoning be spoken of as a triumph? No. I mean, is there no mourning in the home of the bereaved that such blasphemy is permitted?

Jane (*after a moment's pause*)   Perhaps I can understand you now. The time we picked for you was not really one for seeing us at our best.

Olunde   Don't think it was just the war. Before that even started I had plenty of time to study your people. I saw nothing, finally, that gave you the right to pass judgement on other peoples and their ways. Nothing at all.

Jane (*hesitantly*)   Was it the . . . colour thing? I know there is some discrimination.

Olunde   Don't make it so simple, Mrs Pilkings. You make it sound as if when I left, I took nothing at all with me.

Jane   Yes . . . and to tell the truth, only this evening, Simon and I agreed that we never really knew what you left with.

Olunde   Neither did I. But I found out over there. I am grateful to your country for that. And I will never give it up.

Jane   Olunde, please . . . promise me something. Whatever you do, don't throw away what you have started to do. You want to be a doctor. My husband and I believe you will make an excellent one, sympathetic and competent. Don't let anything make you throw away your training.

Olunde (*genuinely surprised*)   Of course not. What a strange idea. I intend to return and complete my training. Once the burial of my father is over.

Jane   Oh, please...!

Olunde   Listen! Come outside. You can't hear anything against that music.

Jane   What is it?

Olunde   The drums. Can you hear the drums? Listen.

The drums come over, still distant but more distinct. There is a change of rhythm, it rises to a crescendo and then, suddenly, it is cut off. After a silence, a new beat begins, slow and resonant.

Olunde   There it's all over.

Jane   You mean he's...

Olunde   Yes, Mrs Pilkings, my father is dead. His will-power has always been enormous; I know he is dead.

Jane (*screams*)   How can you be so callous! So unfeeling! You announce your father's own death like a surgeon looking down on some strange ... stranger's body! You're just a savage like all the rest.

Aide-de-Camp (*rushing out*)   Mrs Pilkings. Mrs Pilkings. (*She breaks down, sobbing.*) Are you all right, Mrs Pilkings?

Olunde   She'll be all right. (*Turns to go.*)

Aide-de-Camp   Who are you? And who the hell asked your opinion?

Olunde   You're quite right, nobody. (*Going.*)

Aide-de-Camp   What the hell! Did you hear me ask you who you were?

Olunde   I have business to attend to.

Aide-de-Camp   I'll give you business in a moment you impudent nigger. Answer my question!

Olunde I have a funeral to arrange. Excuse me. (*Going.*)

Aide-de-Camp I said stop! Orderly!

Jane No, no, don't do that. I'm all right. And for heaven's sake don't act so foolishly. He's a family friend.

Aide-de-Camp Well he'd better learn to answer civil questions when he's asked them. These natives put a suit on and they get high opinions of themselves.

Olunde Can I go now?

Jane No no don't go. I must talk to you. I'm sorry about what I said.

Olunde It's nothing, Mrs Pilkings. And I'm really anxious to go. I couldn't see my father before, it's forbidden for me, his heir and successor, to set eyes on him from the moment of the King's death. But now ... I would like to touch his body while it is still warm.

Jane You will. I promise I shan't keep you long. Only, I couldn't possibly let you go like that. Bob, please excuse us.

Aide-de-Camp If you're sure ...

Jane Of course I'm sure. Something happened to upset me just then, but I'm all right now. Really.

The **Aide-de-Camp** *goes, somewhat reluctantly.*

Olunde I mustn't stay long.

Jane Please, I promise not to keep you. It's just that ... oh you saw yourself what happens to one in this place. The Resident's man thought he was being helpful, that's the way we all react. But I can't go in among that crowd just now and if I stay by myself somebody will come looking for me. Please, just say something for a few moments and then you can go. Just so I can recover myself.

Olunde What do you want me to say?

Jane Your calm acceptance for instance, can you explain

that? It was so unnatural. I don't understand that at all. I feel a need to understand all I can.

Olunde But you explained it yourself. My medical training perhaps. I have seen death too often. And the soldiers who returned from the front, they died on our hands all the time.

Jane No. It has to be more than that. I feel it has to do with the many things we don't really grasp about your people. At least you can explain.

Olunde All these things are part of it. And anyway, my father has been dead in my mind for nearly a month. Ever since I learnt of the King's death. I've lived with my bereavement so long now that I cannot think of him alive. On that journey on the boat, I kept my mind on my duties as the one who must perform the rites over his body. I went through it all again and again in my mind as he himself had taught me. I didn't want to do anything wrong, something which might jeopardise the welfare of my people.

Jane But he had disowned you. When you left he swore publicly you were no longer his son.

Olunde I told you, he was a man of tremendous will. Sometimes that's another way of saying stubborn. But among our people, you don't disown a child just like that. Even if I had died before him I would still be buried like his eldest son. But it's time for me to go.

Jane Thank you. I feel calmer. Don't let me keep you from your duties.

Olunde Goodnight, Mrs Pilkings.

Jane Welcome home.

She holds out her hand. As he takes it footsteps are heard approaching the drive. A short while later a woman's sobbing is also heard.

Pilkings (*off*) Keep them here till I get back. (*He strides into view, reacts at the sight of* **Olunde** *but turns to his wife.*) Thank goodness you're still here.

Jane Simon, what happened?

Pilkings Later Jane, please. Is Bob still here?

Jane Yes, I think so. I'm sure he must be.

Pilkings Try and get him out here as quickly as you can. Tell him it's urgent.

Jane Of course. Oh Simon, you remember . . .

Pilkings Yes yes. I can see who it is. Get Bob out here. (*She runs off.*) At first I thought I was seeing a ghost.

Olunde Mr Pilkings, I appreciate what you tried to do. I want you to believe that. I can tell you it would have been a terrible calamity if you'd succeeded.

Pilkings (*opens his mouth several times, shuts it*) You . . . said what?

Olunde A calamity for us, the entire people.

Pilkings (*sighs*) I see. Hm.

Olunde And now I must go. I must see him before he turns cold.

Pilkings Oh ah . . . em . . . but this is a shock to see you. I mean er thinking all this while you were in England and thanking God for that.

Olunde I came on the mail boat. We travelled in the Prince's convoy.

Pilkings Ah yes, a-ah, hm . . . er well . . .

Olunde Goodnight. I can see you are shocked by the whole business. But you must know by now there are things you cannot understand – or help.

Pilkings Yes. Just a minute. There are armed policemen that way and they have instructions to let no one pass. I suggest you wait a little. I'll er . . . give you an escort.

Olunde That's very kind of you. But do you think it could be quickly arranged.

Pilkings   Of course. In fact, yes, what I'll do is send Bob
over with some men to the er ... place. You can go with
them. Here he comes now. Excuse me a minute.

Aide-de-Camp   Anything wrong sir?

Pilkings (*takes him to one side*)   Listen Bob, that cellar in the
disused annexe of the Residency, you know, where the slaves
were stored before being taken down to the coast ...

Aide-de-Camp   Oh yes, we use it as a storeroom for
broken furniture.

Pilkings   But it's still got the bars on it?

Aide-de-Camp   Oh yes, they are quite intact.

Pilkings   Get the keys please. I'll explain later. And I want
a strong guard over the Residency tonight.

Aide-de-Camp   We have that already. The detachment
from the coast ...

Pilkings   No, I don't want them at the gates of the
Residency. I want you to deploy them at the bottom of the
hill, a long way from the main hall so they can deal with any
situation long before the sound carries to the house.

Aide-de-Camp   Yes of course.

Pilkings   I don't want His Highness alarmed.

Aide-de-Camp   You think the riot will spread here?

Pilkings   It's unlikely but I don't want to take a chance. I
made them believe I was going to lock the man up in my
house, which was what I had planned to do in the first place.
They are probably assailing it by now. I took a roundabout
route here so I don't think there is any danger at all. At least
not before dawn. Nobody is to leave the premises of course –
the native employees I mean. They'll soon smell something is
up and they can't keep their mouths shut.

Aide-de-Camp I'll give instructions at once.

Pilkings I'll take the prisoner down myself. Two policemen will stay with him throughout the night. Inside the cell.

Aide-de-Camp Right sir. (*Salutes and goes off at the double.*)

Pilkings Jane. Bob is coming back in a moment with a detachment. Until he gets back please stay with Olunde. (*He makes an extra warning gesture with his eyes.*)

Olunde Please, Mr Pilkings . . .

Pilkings I hate to be stuffy old son, but we have a crisis on our hands. It has to do with your father's affair if you must know. And it happens also at a time when we have His Highness here. I am responsible for security so you'll simply have to do as I say. I hope that's understood. (*Marches off quickly, in the direction from which he made his first appearance.*)

Olunde What's going on? All this can't be just because he failed to stop my father killing himself.

Jane I honestly don't know. Could it have sparked off a riot?

Olunde No. If he'd succeeded that would be more likely to start the riot. Perhaps there were other factors involved. Was there a chieftaincy dispute?

Jane None that I know of.

Elesin (*an animal bellow from off*) Leave me alone! Is it not enough that you have covered me in shame! White man, take your hand from my body!

Olunde *stands frozen to the spot.* **Jane,** *understanding at last, tries to move him.*

Jane Let's go in. It's getting chilly out here.

Pilkings (*off*) Carry him.

Elesin Give me back the name you have taken away from

me you ghost from the land of the nameless!

Pilkings   Carry him! I can't have a disturbance here. Quickly! stuff up his mouth.

Jane   Oh God! Let's go in. Please Olunde.

Olunde *does not move.*

Elesin   Take your albino's hand from me you . . .

Sounds of a struggle. His voice chokes as he is gagged.

Olunde (*quietly*)   That was my father's voice.

Jane   Oh you poor orphan, what have you come home to?

There is a sudden explosion of rage from off-stage and powerful steps come running up the drive.

Pilkings   You bloody fools, after him!

Immediately **Elesin**, *in handcuffs, comes pounding in the direction of* **Jane** *and* **Olunde**, *followed some moments afterwards by* **Pilkings** *and the constables.* **Elesin**, *confronted by the seeming statue of his son, stops dead.* **Olunde** *stares above his head into the distance. The constables try to grab him.* **Jane** *screams at them.*

Jane   Leave him alone! Simon, tell them to leave him alone.

Pilkings   All right, stand aside you. (*Shrugs.*) Maybe just as well. It might help to calm him down.

For several moments they hold the same position. **Elesin** *moves a step forward, almost as if he's still in doubt.*

Elesin   Olunde? (*He moves his head, inspecting him from side to side.*) Olunde! (*He collapses slowly at* **Olunde**'s *feet.*) Oh son, don't let the sight of your father turn you blind!

Olunde (*he moves for the first time since he heard his voice, brings his head slowly down to look on him*)   I have no father, eater of left-overs.

He walks slowly down the way his father had run. Light fades out on **Elesin**, *sobbing into the ground.*

Scene Five

A wide iron-barred gate stretches almost the whole width of the cell in which **Elesin** *is imprisoned. His wrists are encased in thick iron bracelets, chained together; he stands against the bars, looking out. Seated on the ground to one side on the outside is his recent* **Bride**, *her eyes bent perpetually to the ground. Figures of the two guards can be seen deeper inside the cell, alert to every movement* **Elesin** *makes.* **Pilkings**, *now in a police officer's uniform, enters noiselessly, observes him a while. Then he coughs ostentatiously and approaches. Leans against the bars near a corner, his back to* **Elesin**. *He is obviously trying to fall in mood with him. Some moments' silence.*

Pilkings You seem fascinated by the moon.

Elesin (*after a pause*) Yes, ghostly one. Your twin-brother up there engages my thoughts.

Pilkings It is a beautiful night.

Elesin Is that so?

Pilkings The light on the leaves, the peace of the night...

Elesin The night is not at peace, District Officer.

Pilkings No? I would have said it was. You know, quiet...

Elesin And does quiet mean peace for you?

Pilkings Well, nearly the same thing. Naturally there is a subtle difference...

Elesin The night is not at peace, ghostly one. The world is not at peace. You have shattered the peace of the world for ever. There is no sleep in the world tonight.

Pilkings It is still a good bargain if the world should lose one night's sleep as the price of saving a man's life.

Elesin You did not save my life, District Officer. You destroyed it.

Pilkings Now come on...

Elesin   And not merely my life but the lives of many. The
end of the night's work is not over. Neither this year nor the
next will see it. If I wished you well, I would pray that you
do not stay long enough on our land to see the disaster you
have brought upon us.

Pilkings   Well, I did my duty as I saw it. I have no regrets.

Elesin   No. The regrets of life always come later.

Some moments' pause.

You are waiting for dawn, white man. I hear you saying to
yourself: only so many hours until dawn and then the danger
is over. All I must do is to keep him alive tonight. You don't
quite understand it all but you know that tonight is when
what ought to be must be brought about. I shall ease your
mind even more, ghostly one. It is not an entire night but a
moment of the night, and that moment is past. The moon
was my messenger and guide. When it reached a certain
gateway in the sky, it touched that moment for which my
whole life has been spent in blessings. Even I do not know the
gateway. I have stood here and scanned the sky for a glimpse
of that door but, I cannot see it. Human eyes are useless for a
search of this nature. But in the house of *osugbo*, those who
keep watch through the spirit recognised the moment, they
sent word to me through the voice of our sacred drums to
prepare myself. I heard them and I shed all thoughts of earth.
I began to follow the moon to the abode of the gods ...
servant of the white king, that was when you entered my
chosen place of departure on feet of desecration.

Pilkings   I'm sorry, but we all see our duty differently.

Elesin   I no longer blame you. You stole from me my first-
born, sent him to your country so you could turn him into
something in your own image. Did you plan it all beforehand?
There are moments when it seems part of a larger plan. He
who must follow my footsteps is taken from me, sent across
the ocean. Then, in my turn, I am stopped from fulfilling my
destiny. Did you think it all out before, this plan to push our

world from its course and sever the cord that links us to the great origin?

Pilkings   You don't really believe that. Anyway, if that was my intention with your son, I appear to have failed.

Elesin   You did not fail in the main, ghostly one. We know the roof covers the rafters, the cloth covers blemishes; who would have known that the white skin covered our future, preventing us from seeing the death our enemies had prepared for us. The world is set adrift and its inhabitants are lost. Around them, there is nothing but emptiness.

Pilkings   Your son does not take so gloomy a view.

Elesin   Are you dreaming now, white man? Were you not present at the reunion of shame? Did you not see when the world reversed itself and the father fell before his son, asking forgiveness?

Pilkings   That was in the heat of the moment. I spoke to him and . . . if you want to know, he wishes he could cut out his tongue for uttering the words he did.

Elesin   No. What he said must never be unsaid. The contempt of my own son rescued something of my shame at your hands. You have stopped me in my duty but I know now that I did give birth to a son. Once I mistrusted him for seeking the companionship of those my spirit knew as enemies of our race. Now I understand. One should seek to obtain the secrets of his enemies. He will avenge my shame, white one. His spirit will destroy you and yours.

Pilkings   That kind of talk is hardly called for. If you don't want my consolation . . .

Elesin   No white man, I do not want your consolation.

Pilkings   As you wish. Your son, anyway, sends his consolation. He asks your forgiveness. When I asked him not to despise you his reply was: I cannot judge him, and if I cannot judge him, I cannot despise him. He wants to come to you and say goodbye and to receive your blessing.

Elesin   Goodbye? Is he returning to your land?

Pilkings   Don't you think that's the most sensible thing for him to do? I advised him to leave at once, before dawn, and he agrees that is the right course of action.

Elesin   Yes, it is best. And even if I did not think so, I have lost the father's place of honour. My voice is broken.

Pilkings   Your son honours you. If he didn't he would not ask your blessing.

Elesin   No. Even a thoroughbred is not without pity for the turf he strikes with his hoof. When is he coming?

Pilkings   As soon as the town is a little quieter. I advised it.

Elesin   Yes, white man, I am sure you advised it. You advise all our lives although on the authority of what gods, I do not know.

Pilkings   (*opens his mouth to reply, then appears to change his mind. Turns to go. Hesitates and stops again*)   Before I leave you, may I ask just one thing of you?

Elesin   I am listening.

Pilkings   I wish to ask you to search the quiet of your heart and tell me – do you not find great contradictions in the wisdom of your own race?

Elesin   Make yourself clear, white one.

Pilkings   I have lived among you long enough to learn a saying or two. One came to my mind tonight when I stepped into the market and saw what was going on. You were surrounded by those who egged you on with songs and praises. I thought, are these not the same people who say: the elder grimly approaches heaven and you ask him to bear your greetings yonder; do you really think he makes the journey willingly? After that, I did not hesitate.

A pause. **Elesin** *sighs. Before he can speak a sound of running feet is heard.*

Jane (*off*) Simon! Simon!

Pilkings What on earth. . . ! (*Runs off.*)

Elesin turns to his new wife, gazes on her for some moments.

Elesin My young bride, did you hear the ghostly one? You sit and sob in your silent heart but say nothing to all this. First I blamed the white man, then I blamed my gods for deserting me. Now I feel I want to blame you for the mystery of the sapping of my will. But blame is a strange peace offering for a man to bring a world he has deeply wronged, and to its innocent dwellers. Oh little mother, I have taken countless women in my life but you were more than a desire of the flesh. I needed you as the abyss across which my body must be drawn, I filled it with earth and dropped my seed in it at the moment of preparedness for my crossing. You were the final gift of the living to their emissary to the land of the ancestors, and perhaps your warmth and youth brought new insights of this world to me and turned my feet leaden on this side of the abyss. For I confess to you, daughter, my weakness came not merely from the abomination of the white man who came violently into my fading presence, there was also a weight of longing on my earth-held limbs. I would have shaken it off, already my foot had begun to lift but then, the white ghost entered and all was defiled.

Approaching voices of **Pilkings** *and his wife.*

Jane Oh Simon, you will let her in won't you?

Pilkings I really wish you'd stop interfering.

They come into view. **Jane** *is in a dressing-gown.* **Pilkings** *is holding a note to which he refers from time to time.*

Jane Good gracious, I didn't initiate this. I was sleeping quietly, or trying to anyway, when the servant brought it. It's not my fault if one can't sleep undisturbed even in the Residency.

Pilkings He'd have done the same thing if we were sleeping at home so don't sidetrack the issue. He knows he can get round you or he wouldn't send you the petition in the first place.

Jane Be fair Simon. After all he was thinking of your own interests. He is grateful you know, you seem to forget that. He feels he owes you something.

Pilkings I just wish they'd leave this man alone tonight, that's all.

Jane Trust him Simon. He's pledged his word it will all go peacefully.

Pilkings Yes, and that's the other thing. I don't like being threatened.

Jane Threatened? (*Takes the note.*) I didn't spot any threat.

Pilkings It's there. Veiled, but it's there. The only way to prevent serious rioting tomorrow – what a cheek!

Jane I don't think he's threatening you Simon.

Pilkings He's picked up the idiom all right. Wouldn't surprise me if he's been mixing with commies or anarchists over there. The phrasing sounds too good to be true. Damn! If only the Prince hadn't picked this time for his visit.

Jane Well, even so Simon, what have you got to lose? You don't want a riot on your hands, not with the Prince here.

Pilkings (*going up to* **Elesin**) Let's see what he has to say. Chief Elesin, there is yet another person who wants to see you. As she is not a next-of-kin I don't really feel obliged to let her in. But your son sent a note with her, so it's up to you.

Elesin I know who that must be. So she found out your hiding-place. Well, it was not difficult. My stench of shame is so strong, it requires no hunter's dog to follow it.

Pilkings If you don't want to see her, just say so and I'll send her packing.

Elesin Why should I not want to see her? Let her come. I have no more holes in my rag of shame. All is laid bare.

Pilkings   I'll bring her in. (*Goes off.*)

Jane (*hesitates, then goes to* **Elesin**)   Please, try and understand. Everything my husband did was for the best.

Elesin (*he gives her a long strange stare, as if he is trying to understand who she is*)   You are the wife of the District Officer?

Jane   Yes. My name, is Jane.

Elesin   That is my wife sitting down there. You notice how still and silent she sits? My business is with your husband.

Pilkings *returns with* **Iyaloja**.

Pilkings   Here she is. Now first I want your word of honour that you will try nothing foolish.

Elesin   Honour? White one, did you say you wanted my word of honour?

Pilkings   I know you to be an honourable man. Give me your word of honour you will receive nothing from her.

Elesin   But I am sure you have searched her clothing as you would never dare touch your own mother. And there are these two lizards of yours who roll their eyes even when I scratch.

Pilkings   And I shall be sitting on that tree trunk watching even how you blink. Just the same I want your word that you will not let her pass anything to you.

Elesin   You have my honour already. It is locked up in that desk in which you will put away your report of this night's events. Even the honour of my people you have taken already; it is tied together with those papers of treachery which make you masters in this land.

Pilkings   All right. I am trying to make things easy but if you must bring in politics we'll have to do it the hard way. Madam, I want you to remain along this line and move no nearer to the cell door. Guards! (*They spring to attention.*) If she moves beyond this point, blow your whistle. Come on Jane. (*They go off.*)

Iyaloja How boldly the lizard struts before the pigeon when it was the eagle itself he promised us he would confront.

Elesin I don't ask you to take pity on me Iyaloja. You have a message for me or you would not have come. Even if it is the curses of the world, I shall listen.

Iyaloja You made so bold with the servant of the white king who took your side against death. I must tell your brother chiefs when I return how bravely you waged war against him. Especially with words.

Elesin I more than deserve your scorn.

Iyaloja (*with sudden anger*) I warned you, if you must leave a seed behind, be sure it is not tainted with the curses of the world. Who are you to open a new life when you dared not open the door to a new existence? I say who are you to make so bold? (*The* **Bride** *sobs and* **Iyaloja** *notices her. Her contempt noticeably increases as she turns back to* **Elesin**.) Oh you self-vaunted stem of the plantain, how hollow it all proves. The pith is gone in the parent stem, so how will it prove with the new shoot? How will it go with that earth that bears it? Who are you to bring this abomination on us!

Elesin My powers deserted me. My charms, my spells, even my voice lacked strength when I made to summon the powers that would lead me over the last measure of earth into the land of the fleshless. You saw it, Iyaloja. You saw me struggle to retrieve my will from the power of the stranger whose shadow fell across the doorway and left me floundering and blundering in a maze I had never before encountered. My senses were numbed when the touch of cold iron came upon my wrists. I could do nothing to save myself.

Iyaloja You have betrayed us. We fed you sweetmeats such as we hoped awaited you on the other side. But you said No, I must eat the world's left-overs. We said you were the hunter who brought the quarry down; to you belonged the vital portions of the game. No, you said, I am the hunter's dog and I shall eat the entrails of the game and the faeces of the hunter. We said you were the hunter returning home in triumph, a slain buffalo pressing down on his neck; you said Wait, I first must turn up this cricket hole with my toes. We said yours was the doorway at which we first spy the tapper when he comes down from the tree, yours was the blessing of the twilight wine, the purl that brings night spirits out of doors to steal their portion before the light of day. We said yours was the body of wine whose burden shakes the tapper like a sudden gust on his perch. You said, No, I am content to lick the dregs from each calabash when the drinkers are done. We said, the dew on earth's surface was for you to wash your feet along the slopes of honour. You said No, I shall step in the vomit of cats and the droppings of mice; I shall fight them for the left-overs of the world.

Elesin   Enough Iyaloja, enough.

Iyaloja   We called you leader and oh, how you led us on. What we have no intention of eating should not be held to the nose.

Elesin   Enough, enough. My shame is heavy enough.

Iyaloja   Wait. I came with a burden.

Elesin   You have more than discharged it.

Iyaloja   I wish I could pity you.

Elesin   I need neither pity nor the pity of the world. I need understanding. Even I need to understand. You were present at my defeat. You were part of the beginnings. You brought about the renewal of my tie to earth, you helped in the binding of the cord.

Iyaloja   I gave you warning. The river which fills up before our eyes does not sweep us away in its flood.

Elesin   What were warnings beside the moist contact of living earth between my fingers? What were warnings beside the renewal of famished embers lodged eternally in the heart of man. But even that, even if it overwhelmed one with a thousandfold temptations to linger a little while, a man could overcome it. It is when the alien hand pollutes the source of will, when a stranger force of violence shatters the mind's calm resolution, this is when a man is made to commit the awful treachery of relief, commit in his thought the unspeakable blasphemy of seeing the hand of the gods in this alien rupture of his world. I know it was this thought that killed me, sapped my powers and turned me into an infant in the hands of unnamable strangers. I made to utter my spells anew but my tongue merely rattled in my mouth. I fingered hidden charms and the contact was damp; there was no spark left to sever the life-strings that should stretch from every finger-tip. My will was squelched in the spittle of an alien race, and all because I had committed this blasphemy of thought – that there might be the hand of the gods in a stranger's intervention.

Iyaloja   Explain it how you will, I hope it brings you peace of mind. The bush-rat fled his rightful cause, reached the market and set up a lamentation. 'Please save me!' – are these fitting words to hear from an ancestral mask? 'There's a wild beast at my heels' is not becoming language from a hunter.

Elesin   May the world forgive me.

Iyaloja   I came with a burden I said. It approaches the gates which are so well guarded by those jackals whose spittle will from this day be on your food and drink. But first, tell me, you who were once Elesin Oba, tell me, you who know so well the cycle of the plantain: is it the parent shoot which withers to give sap to the younger or, does your wisdom see it running the other way?

Elesin   I don't see your meaning Iyaloja?

Iyaloja   Did I ask you for a meaning? I asked a question. Whose trunk withers to give sap to the other? The parent shoot or the younger?

Elesin   The parent.

Iyaloja   Ah. So you do know that. There are sights in this world which say different Elesin. There are some who choose to reverse the cycle of our being. Oh, you emptied bark that the world once saluted for a pith-laden being, shall I tell you what the gods have claimed of you?

In her agitation she steps beyond the line indicated by **Pilkings** *and the air is rent by piercing whistles. The two guards also leap forward and place safeguarding hands on* **Elesin**. **Iyaloja** *stops, astonished.* **Pilkings** *comes racing in, followed by* **Jane**.

Pilkings   What is it? Did they try something?

Guard   She stepped beyond the line.

Elesin (*in a broken voice*)   Let her alone. She meant no harm.

Iyaloja   Oh Elesin, see what you've become. Once you had no need to open your mouth in explanation because evil-smelling goats, itchy of hand and foot, had lost their senses. And it was a brave man indeed who dared lay hands on you because Iyaloja stepped from one side of the earth onto another. Now look at the spectacle of your life. I grieve for you.

Pilkings   I think you'd better leave. I doubt you have done him much good by coming here. I shall make sure you are not allowed to see him again. In any case we are moving him to a different place before dawn, so don't bother to come back.

Iyaloja   We foresaw that. Hence the burden I trudged here to lay beside your gates.

Pilkings   What was that you said?

Iyaloja   Didn't our son explain? Ask that one. He knows what it is. At least we hope the man we once knew as Elesin remembers the lesser oaths he need not break.

Pilkings   Do you know what she is talking about?

Elesin   Go to the gates, ghostly one. Whatever you find there, bring it to me.

Iyaloja Not yet. It drags behind me on the slow, weary feet of women. Slow as it is Elesin, it has long overtaken you. It rides ahead of your laggard will.

Pilkings What is she saying now? Christ! Must your people forever speak in riddles?

Elesin It will come white man, it will come. Tell your men at the gates to let it through.

Pilkings (*dubiously*) I'll have to see what it is.

Iyaloja You will. (*Passionately*.) But this is one oath he cannot shirk. White one, you have a king here, a visitor from your land. We know of his presence here. Tell me, were he to die would you leave his spirit roaming restlessly on the surface of earth? Would you bury him here among those you consider less than human? In your land have you no ceremonies of the dead?

Pilkings Yes. But we don't make our chiefs commit suicide to keep him company.

Iyaloja Child, I have not come to help your understanding. (*Points to* **Elesin**.) This is the man whose weakened understanding holds us in bondage to you. But ask him if you wish. He knows the meaning of a king's passage; he was not born yesterday. He knows the peril to the race when our dead father, who goes as intermediary, waits and waits and knows he is betrayed. He knows when the narrow gate was opened and he knows it will not stay for laggards who drag their feet in dung and vomit, whose lips are reeking of the left-overs of lesser men. He knows he has condemned our King to wander in the void of evil with beings who are enemies of life.

Pilkings Yes er ... but look here ...

Iyaloja What we ask is little enough. Let him release our King so he can ride on homewards alone. The messenger is on his way on the backs of women. Let him send word through the heart that is folded up within the bolt. It is the least of all his oaths, it is the easiest fulfilled.

The **Aide-de-Camp** *runs in.*

Pilkings Bob?

Aide-de-Camp Sir, there's a group of women chanting up the hill.

Pilkings (*rounding on* **Iyaloja**) If you people want trouble . . .

Jane Simon, I think that's what Olunde referred to in his letter.

Pilkings He knows damned well I can't have a crowd here! Damn it, I explained the delicacy of my position to him. I think it's about time I got him out of town. Bob, send a car and two or three soldiers to bring him in. I think the sooner he takes his leave of his father and gets out the better.

Iyaloja Save your labour white one. If it is the father of your prisoner you want, Olunde, he who until this night we knew as Elesin's son, he comes soon himself to take his leave. He has sent the women ahead, so let them in.

Pilkings *remains undecided.*

Aide-de-Camp What do we do about the invasion? We can still stop them far from here.

Pilkings What do they look like?

Aide-de-Camp They're not many. And they seem quite peaceful.

Pilkings No men?

Aide-de-Camp Mm, two or three at the most.

Jane Honestly, Simon, I'd trust Olunde. I don't think he'll deceive you about their intentions.

Pilkings He'd better not. All right then, let them in Bob. Warn them to control themselves. Then hurry Olunde here. Make sure he brings his baggage because I'm not returning him into town.

Aide-de-Camp Very good, sir. (*Goes.*)

Pilkings (*to* **Iyaloja**)   I hope you understand that if anything goes wrong it will be on your head. My men have orders to shoot at the first sign of trouble.

Iyaloja   To prevent one death you will actually make other deaths? Ah, great is the wisdom of the white race. But have no fear. Your Prince will sleep peacefully. So at long last will ours. We will disturb you no further, servant of the white King. Just let Elesin fulfil his oath and we will retire home and pay homage to our King.

Jane   I believe her Simon, don't you?

Pilkings   Maybe.

Elesin   Have no fear ghostly one. I have a message to send my King and then you have nothing more to fear.

Iyaloja   Olunde would have done it. The chiefs asked him to speak the words but he said no, not while you lived.

Elesin   Even from the depths to which my spirit has sunk, I find some joy that this little has been left to me.

The **Women** *enter, intoning the dirge 'Ale le le' and swaying from side to side. On their shoulders is borne a longish object roughly like a cylindrical bolt, covered in cloth. They set it down on the spot where* **Iyaloja** *had stood earlier, and form a semi-circle round it. The* **Praise-Singer** *and drummer stand on the inside of the semi-circle but the drum is not used at all. The drummer intones under the* **Praise-Singer***'s invocations.*

Pilkings (*as they enter*)   What is *that*?

Iyaloja   The burden you have made white one, but we bring it in peace.

Pilkings   I said *what* is it?

Elesin   White man, you must let me out. I have a duty to perform.

Pilkings   I most certainly will not.

Elesin   There lies the courier of my King. Let me out so I can perform what is demanded of me.

Pilkings   You'll do what you need to do from inside there or not at all. I've gone as far as I intend to with this business.

Elesin   The worshipper who lights a candle in your church to bear a message to his god bows his head and speaks in a whisper to the flame. Have I not seen it ghostly one? His voice does not ring out to the world. Mine are no words for anyone's ears. They are not words even for the bearers of this load. They are words I must speak secretly, even as my father whispered them in my ears and I in the ears of my first-born. I cannot shout them to the wind and the open night-sky.

Jane   Simon . . .

Pilkings   Don't interfere. Please!

Iyaloja   They have slain the favourite horse of the King and slain his dog. They have borne them from pulse to pulse centre of the land receiving prayers for their King. But the rider has chosen to stay behind. Is it too much to ask that he speak his heart to heart of the waiting courier? (**Pilkings** *turns his back on her.*) So be it, Elesin Oba, you see how even the mere leavings are denied you. (*She gestures to the* **Praise-Singer**.)

Praise-Singer   Elesin Oba! I call you by that name only this last time. Remember when I said, if you cannot come, tell my horse. (*Pause.*) What? I cannot hear you? I said, if you cannot come, whisper in the ears of my horse. Is your tongue severed from the roots? Elesin? I can hear no response. I said, if there are boulders you cannot climb, mount my horse's back, this spotless black stallion, he'll bring you over them. (*Pauses.*) Elesin Oba, once you had a tongue that darted like a drummer's stick. I said, if you get lost my dog will track a path to me. My memory fails me but I think you replied: My feet have found the path, Alafin.

The dirge rises and falls.

I said at the last, if evil hands hold you back, just tell my horse there is weight on the hem of your smock. I dare not wait too long.

The dirge rises and falls.

There lies the swiftest ever messenger of a king, so set me free with the errand of your heart. There lie the head and heart of the favourite of the gods, whisper in his ears. Oh my companion, if you had followed when you should, we would not say that the horse preceded its rider. If you had followed when it was time, we would not say the dog has raced beyond and left his master behind. If you had raised your will to cut the thread of life at the summons of the drums, we would not say your mere shadow fell across the gateway and took its owner's place at the banquet. But the hunter, laden with slain buffalo, stayed to root in the cricket's hole with his toes. What now is left? If there is a dearth of bats, the pigeon must serve us for the offering. Speak the words over your shadow which must now serve in your place.

Elesin   I cannot approach. Take off the cloth. I shall speak my message from heart to heart of silence.

Iyaloja (*moves forward and removes the covering*)   Your courier Elesin, cast your eyes on the favoured companion of the King.

Rolled up in the mat, his head and feet showing at either end, is the body of **Olunde**.

There lies the honour of your household and of our race. Because he could not bear to let honour fly out of doors, he stopped it with his life. The son has proved the father, Elesin, and there is nothing left in your mouth to gnash but infant gums.

Praise-Singer   Elesin, we placed the reins of the world in your hands yet you watched it plunge over the edge of the bitter precipice. You sat with folded arms while evil strangers tilted the world from its course and crashed it beyond the edge of emptiness – you muttered, there is little that one man can do, you left us floundering in a blind future. Your heir has taken the burden on himself. What the end will be, we are not gods to tell. But this young shoot has poured its sap into the parent stalk, and we know this is not the way of life. Our world is tumbling in the void of strangers, Elesin.

Elesin *has stood rock-still, his knuckles taut on the bars, his eyes glued to the body of his son. The stillness seizes and paralyses everyone, including* **Pilkings** *who has turned to look. Suddenly* **Elesin** *flings one arm round his neck, once, and with the loop of the chain, strangles himself in a swift, decisive pull. The guards rush forward to stop him but they are only in time to let his body down.* **Pilkings** *has leapt to the door at the same time and struggles with the lock. He rushes within, fumbles with the handcuffs and unlocks them, raises the body to a sitting position while he tries to give resuscitation. The* **Women** *continue their dirge, unmoved by the sudden event.*

Iyaloja   Why do you strain yourself? Why do you labour at tasks for which no one, not even the man lying there, would give you thanks? He is gone at last into the passage but oh, how late it all is. His son will feast on the meat and throw him bones. The passage is clogged with droppings from the King's stallion; he will arrive all stained in dung.

Pilkings (*in a tired voice*)   Was this what you wanted?

Iyaloja   No child, it is what you brought to be, you who play with strangers' lives, who even usurp the vestments of our dead, yet believe that the stain of death will not cling to you. The gods demanded only the old expired plantain but you cut down the sap-laden shoot to feed your pride. There is your board, filled to overflowing. Feast on it. (*She screams at him suddenly, seeing that* **Pilkings** *is about to close* **Elesin**'s *staring eyes.*) Let him alone! However sunk he was in debt he is no pauper's carrion abandoned on the road. Since when have strangers donned clothes of indigo before the bereaved cries out his loss?

She turns to the **Bride** *who has remained motionless throughout.*

Child.

The girl takes up a little earth, walks calmly into the cell and closes **Elesin**'s *eyes. She then pours some earth over each eyelid and comes out* *again.*

Iyaloja   Now forget the dead, forget even the living. Turn your mind only to the unborn.

She goes off, accompanied by the **Bride**. *The dirge rises in volume and the* **Women** *continue their sway. Lights fade to a blackout.*

Notes

and dangerous path down which it is the role of the
King's Horseman to lead his master.

yams: a large kind of tuber, the staple food of the
Yoruba, farmed by men and of immense significance in
Yoruba culture.

14   *calabash*: a hollowed-out drinking vessel or container,
made from the sun-hardened skin of the calabash fruit.

16   *sanyan*: a richly valued woven cloth.

18   *iroko tree*: a tree widespread in southern Nigeria.

19   *Oka*: a python.

Baba O!: 'Oh Father!'

cola: a nut widely used in West Africa, and slowly
chewed. It is often taken as a gift.

Ogun: One of the most powerful of the Yoruba pantheon
of gods, and the god with whom Soyinka most closely
identifies. He is the god of creation and destruction, the
god of metal and of roads. Most significantly here, he is
the god who dared to forge a way across the transitional
gulf, by force of his tremendous will, to re-link the
worlds of gods and men after they had become
separated.

21   *plantain*: a tuber commonly grown and eaten.

23   *awusa nut*: a northern Nigerian nut.

24   *agbada*: a loose long robe worn by men.

Scene Two

24   *District Officer*: British colonial administrators – their job
was to keep law and order and maintain British rule in
their district. They had enormous powers over the local
population and each covered a large area.

Native Administration: under the system of indirect rule
operated by the British in West Africa certain powers
were devolved to local indigenous hierarchies, often led
by chiefs approved or appointed by the British. These
powers included running a local police force.

26   *egungun*: these masks, or costumes, cover the whole body.
They are brought out on ceremonial occasions when the

men wearing them represent the spirits of the ancestors. The *egungun* masks are a central part of Yoruba religious rites.

juju: the practice of traditional magic.

32   *Joseph. What's the drumming about?*: Joseph would be able to hear, literally, the message of the talking drums. Yoruba is a tonal language so words alter meaning according to their pitch. By using different pitches and rhythms of words and speech the drums can be made to speak.

missionaries: the missionaries were a central part of the European colonisation of Africa. They imposed Western values via the medium of Christianity and brought Western education to large parts of Africa. They remained largely ignorant of indigenous cultural and spiritual beliefs and practices.

Scene Three

43   *In his hands a white velvet cloth*: the cloth is stained with blood from the breaking of the bride's hymen. This proves she was a virgin, an important consideration in many traditional societies. Without this proof her honour would be in doubt.

47   *It takes an Elesin to die the death of death*: the Elesin must die willingly and in full knowledge of what he does and where he goes, and thereby conquer the fear of death. He thus keeps the road between the worlds clear for his king, and by extension for the people, maintaining the way and the balance between the worlds.

48   *gbedu*: a deep-timbred royal drum.

osugbo: secret 'executive' cult of the Yoruba; its meeting-place.

harmattan: a West African wind, bringing dust from the Sahara.

Scene Four

49   *A masque*: not to be confused with West African

masquing traditions (see note on *egungun*, above).
Masques in Europe were formal dance-stories in
elaborate costume. This scene makes an obvious contrast
with the previous trance-dance of Elesin, pointing up the
emptiness of European rituals in contrast to Elesin's
dance of death and redemption.

Resident: the British official a grade higher than a District
Officer.

59   *newsreels*: in this pre-television time newsreels were shown
regularly in cinemas.

64   *that cellar in the disused annexe of the Residency, you know, where
the slaves were stored before being taken down to the coast*: West
Africa was the centre of the slave trade which took
slaves to work on the plantations in America. Holding
Elesin in the conditions in which slaves were held,
complete with manacles, is an ironic touch which is not
registered by the insensitive Pilkings.

66   *albino's hand*: an albino is a person born without
pigmentation. To call a white man an albino is a term
of abuse.

I have no father, eater of left-overs: in a reversal of Elesin's
earlier casting-off of his son for betraying tradition and
going to England, Olunde now casts off his father who
has failed in the central duty and meaning of his life.
'Eater of left-overs' harks back to various references in
the first scene, as when Elesin says (p. 14) 'A life that
will outlive / Fame and friendship begs another name'
and forwards to Scene Five when Iyaloja accuses Elesin
of eating left-overs.

Scene Five

67   *ghostly one*: white men were often seen as ghosts or spirits,
unnatural in their light skin colour.

You have shattered the peace of the world for ever: the natural
order of the Yoruba world has been broken, and this
leaves the way open for many possible calamities.

69   *the cord that links us to the great origin*: according to Yoruba belief, all life is linked, as is all time, and maintaining that linkage and balance is central to the well-being of the world.

71   *I have taken countless women*: traditional leaders had many wives and concubines.

78   *He knows he has condemned our King to wander in the void of evil with beings who are enemies of life*: without his Horseman the King has no guide in the dangerous passage between the worlds of life and death.

82   *The son has proved the father, Elesin*: Olunde has taken Elesin's place by killing himself in an effort to set things right, and the son thereby becomes the father. However, since this death was not committed in the right way or at the right time there is no guarantee that Olunde will be able to carry out the role of Horseman and set matters straight.

84   *Now forget the dead, forget even the living. Turn your mind only to the unborn*: the bride carries Elesin's child who may be a hope for the future. In Yoruba belief, the unborn are as real as the living and the ancestors. They are part of the unity of creation.

Questions for further study

1 'In *Death and the King's Horseman* Soyinka explores ideas on leadership, tradition and the gulf between peoples.' Discuss.

2 Comment on the importance of Iyaloja and Jane Pilkings as they affect the action of the play and our perception of the male characters.

3 Soyinka is said to be fascinated by the power of the human will. In what ways is this made apparent in *Death and the King's Horseman*?

4 Discuss the ways in which the concept of 'honour' is treated in *Death and the King's Horseman*.

5 In what ways is the performance of ritual important to an understanding of *Death and the King's Horseman*?

6 'Soyinka resists simple black and white portrayal of characters and situations because that is not the way he sees the world.' Does *Death and the King's Horseman* seem to you to bear this out?

7 Comment on the portrayal of the role of Olunde in *Death and the King's Horseman*.

8 Compare and contrast the effects achieved by the different kinds of dramatic speech accorded to the Africans and the British in *Death and the King's Horseman*.

9 'The tragic ending to *Death and the King's Horseman* is too contrived to be credible', 'The tragic ending to *Death and the King's Horseman* has the dramatic inevitability of great drama'. Which of these two views would you support and why?

10 In what ways does Soyinka use myth and history to interrogate the contemporary world of Nigeria?

11 'Soyinka's is a Yoruba-inspired vision which sees no division between the spiritual, the political and the

personal.' In what ways and to what effect does *Death and the King's Horseman* demonstrate this?

12 Does Soyinka's apparent concern with 'the exceptional individual' mean that he tends to treat certain characters rather unfairly from our 'democratic' point of view?

13 Given the way in which European wars have involved the African continent and that the action of *Death and the King's Horseman* is based on events which take place in 1945, how might this affect ways in which we read the play?

14 'In *Death and the King's Horseman* Soyinka examines the difficulties of reconciling hedonism and earthly power with the resolve to serve one's community through conscious sacrifice.' Discuss.

15 According to Soyinka, *Death and the King's Horseman* was inspired by an image of Winston Churchill which reminded him 'of the strange byways [of] our history' and 'of the colonial intrusion'. Does this deny his claim elsewhere that the play is not concerned with a clash of cultures?

16 Soyinka describes the basic need for any production of *Death and the King's Horseman* to realise 'the difficult and risky task of eliciting the play's threnodic essence'. What do you think he means and how might one go about achieving this?

17 *Death and the King's Horseman* has been described as a political parable whose aim is to warn leaders against being seduced by the attractions of wealth, lust and power. To what extent would you agree and why?

18 'The Colonial Factor is [. . .] a catalytic incident merely. The confrontation in the play is largely metaphysical, contained in the human vehicle which is Elesin and the universe of the Yoruba mind – the world of the living, the dead and the unborn, and the numinous passage which links all: transition' (Wole Soyinka). Comment on *Death and the King's Horseman* in the light of this statement.

19 Bearing in mind that this play's date of publication (1975) predates the AIDS epidemic in Africa, does this qualify

our view of a play which seems to celebrate human
sexuality and even death itself?

20 Soyinka is on record as saying that *Death and the King's
Horseman* 'can be fully realised only through an evocation
of music from the abyss of transition'. What do you think
he means and how might one go about achieving this in
a production?

Methuen Drama Student Editions

Jean Anouilh *Antigone* • John Arden *Serjeant Musgrave's Dance*
Alan Ayckbourn *Confusions* • Aphra Behn *The Rover* • Edward Bond
Lear • *Saved* • Bertolt Brecht *The Caucasian Chalk Circle* • *Fear and
Misery in the Third Reich* • *The Good Person of Szechwan* • *Life of Galileo* •
Mother Courage and her Children • *The Resistible Rise of Arturo Ui* • *The
Threepenny Opera* • Anton Chekhov *The Cherry Orchard* • *The Seagull* •
Three Sisters • *Uncle Vanya* • Caryl Churchill *Serious Money* • *Top Girls*
• Shelagh Delaney *A Taste of Honey* • Euripides *Elektra* • *Medea* •
Dario Fo *Accidental Death of an Anarchist* • Michael Frayn *Copenhagen*
• John Galsworthy *Strife* • Nikolai Gogol *The Government Inspector* •
Robert Holman *Across Oka* • Henrik Ibsen *A Doll's House* • *Ghosts* •
Hedda Gabler • Charlotte Keatley *My Mother Said I Never Should* •
Bernard Kops *Dreams of Anne Frank* • Federico García Lorca *Blood
Wedding* • *Doña Rosita the Spinster* (bilingual edition) • *The House of
Bernarda Alba* • (bilingual edition) • *Yerma* (bilingual edition) • David
Mamet *Glengarry Glen Ross* • *Oleanna* • Patrick Marber *Closer* • John
Marston *Malcontent* • Martin McDonagh *The Lieutenant of Inishmore* •
Joe Orton *Loot* • Luigi Pirandello *Six Characters in Search of an Author*
• Mark Ravenhill *Shopping and F***ing* • Willy Russell *Blood Brothers*
• *Educating Rita* • Sophocles *Antigone* • *Oedipus the King* • Wole
Soyinka *Death and the King's Horseman* • Shelagh Stephenson *The
Memory of Water* • August Strindberg *Miss Julie* • J. M. Synge *The
Playboy of the Western World* • Theatre Workshop *Oh What a Lovely
War* Timberlake Wertenbaker *Our Country's Good* • Arnold Wesker
The Merchant • Oscar Wilde *The Importance of Being Earnest* •
Tennessee Williams *A Streetcar Named Desire* • *The Glass Menagerie*

Title	Author	ISBN
Antigone	Jean Anouilh	9780413308603
The Hostage	Brendan Behan	9780413311900
A Man for All Seasons	Robert Bolt	9780413703804
Saved	Edward Bond	9780413313607
The Caucasian Chalk Circle	Bertolt Brecht	9780413308504
Fear and Misery in the Third Reich		9780413772664
The Good Person of Szechwan		9780413582409
Life of Galileo		9780413763808
The Messingkauf Dialogues		9780413388902
Mother Courage and Her Children		9780413412904
Mr Puntila and His Man Matti		9781408100707
The Resistible Rise of Arturo Ui		9781408111499
Rise and Fall of the City of Mahagonny		9780713686746
The Threepenny Opera		9780413390301
Road	Jim Cartwright	9780413623904
Two And Bed		9780413683304 (due 2009)
Serious Money	Caryl Churchill	9780413641908
Top Girls		9780413554802
Blithe Spirit	Noel Coward	9780413771971
Hay Fever		9780413540904
Present Laughter		9781408101483
Private Lives		9780413744906
The Vortex		9780413773098
A Taste of Honey	Shelagh Delaney	9780413316806
Accidental Death of an Anarchist	Dario Fo	9780413771575
Copenhagen	Michael Frayn	9780413724908 (due 2009)
A Raisin in the Sun	Lorraine Hansberry	9780413762405 (due 2009)
Beautiful Thing	Jonathan Harvey	9780413710307
Glengarry Glen Ross	David Mamet	9780413554208
Oleanna		9780413626202
Speed-the-Plow		9780413192806
Closer	Patrick Marber	9780413709509
Dealer's Choice		9780413714909 (due 2009)
Woza Albert	Percy Mtwa	9780413530004 (due 2009)
Entertaining Mr Sloane	Joe Orton	9780413413406
Loot		9780413451804
What the Butler Saw		9780413366801
Shopping and F***ing	Mark Ravenhill	9780413712400
Blood Brothers	Willy Russell	9780413767707 (due 2009)
Educating Rita		9780413767905 (due 2009)
Stags and Hens		9780413767806 (due 2009)
Crime Passionnel	Jean-Paul Sartre	9780413310101
Death and the King's Horseman	Wole Soyinka	9780413333605
Oh, What a Lovely War	Theatre Workshop	9780413302106
Spring Awakening	Frank Wedekind	9780413476203 (due 2009)
Our Country's Good	Timberlake Wertenbaker	9780413659002

Methuen Drama Contemporary Dramatists

include

John Arden (two volumes)
Arden & D'Arcy
Peter Barnes (three volumes)
Sebastian Barry
Dermot Bolger
Edward Bond (eight volumes)
Howard Brenton
  (two volumes)
Richard Cameron
Jim Cartwright
Caryl Churchill (two volumes)
Sarah Daniels (two volumes)
Nick Darke
David Edgar (three volumes)
David Eldridge
Ben Elton
Dario Fo (two volumes)
Michael Frayn (three volumes)
John Godber (three volumes)
Paul Godfrey
David Greig
John Guare
Lee Hall (two volumes)
Peter Handke
Jonathan Harvey
  (two volumes)
Declan Hughes
Terry Johnson (three volumes)
Sarah Kane
Barrie Keefe
Bernard-Marie Koltès
  (two volumes)
Franz Xaver Kroetz
David Lan
Bryony Lavery
Deborah Levy
Doug Lucie

David Mamet (four volumes)
Martin McDonagh
Duncan McLean
Anthony Minghella
  (two volumes)
Tom Murphy (five volumes)
Phyllis Nagy
Anthony Neilson
Philip Osment
Gary Owen
Louise Page
Stewart Parker (two volumes)
Joe Penhall
Stephen Poliakoff
  (three volumes)
David Rabe
Mark Ravenhill
Christina Reid
Philip Ridley
Willy Russell
Eric-Emmanuel Schmitt
Ntozake Shange
Sam Shepard (two volumes)
Wole Soyinka (two volumes)
Simon Stephens
Shelagh Stephenson
David Storey (three volumes)
Sue Townsend
Judy Upton
Michel Vinaver
  (two volumes)
Arnold Wesker (two volumes)
Michael Wilcox
Roy Williams (two volumes)
Snoo Wilson (two volumes)
David Wood (two volumes)
Victoria Wood

Methuen Drama World Classics

include

Jean Anouilh (two volumes)
Brendan Behan
Aphra Behn
Bertolt Brecht (eight volumes)
Büchner
Bulgakov
Calderón
Čapek
Anton Chekhov
Noël Coward (eight volumes)
Feydeau
Eduardo De Filippo
Max Frisch
John Galsworthy
Gogol
Gorky (two volumes)
Harley Granville Barker
  (two volumes)
Victor Hugo
Henrik Ibsen (six volumes)
Jarry

Lorca (three volumes)
Marivaux
Mustapha Matura
David Mercer (two volumes)
Arthur Miller (five volumes)
Molière
Musset
Peter Nichols (two volumes)
Joe Orton
A. W. Pinero
Luigi Pirandello
Terence Rattigan
  (two volumes)
W. Somerset Maugham
  (two volumes)
August Strindberg
  (three volumes)
J. M. Synge
Ramón del Valle-Inclán
Frank Wedekind
Oscar Wilde

Methuen Drama Classical Greek Dramatists

Aeschylus Plays: One
(Persians, Seven Against Thebes, Suppliants,
Prometheus Bound)

Aeschylus Plays: Two
(Oresteia: Agamemnon, Libation-Bearers, Eumenides)

Aristophanes Plays: One
(Acharnians, Knights, Peace, Lysistrata)

Aristophanes Plays: Two
(Wasps, Clouds, Birds, Festival Time, Frogs)

Aristophanes & Menander: New Comedy
(Women in Power, Wealth, The Malcontent,
The Woman from Samos)

Euripides Plays: One
(Medea, The Phoenician Women, Bacchae)

Euripides Plays: Two
(Hecuba, The Women of Troy, Iphigeneia at Aulis,
Cyclops)

Euripides Plays: Three
(Alkestis, Helen, Ion)

Euripides Plays: Four
(Elektra, Orestes, Iphigeneia in Tauris)

Euripides Plays: Five
(Andromache, Herakles' Children, Herakles)

Euripides Plays: Six
(Hippolytos, Suppliants, Rhesos)

Sophocles Plays: One
(Oedipus the King, Oedipus at Colonus, Antigone)

Sophocles Plays: Two
(Ajax, Women of Trachis, Electra, Philoctetes)

For a complete catalogue of Methuen Drama titles
write to:

Methuen Drama
36 Soho Square
London
W1D 3QY

or you can visit our website at:

www.methuendrama.com